BRISTOL AIRCRAFT

A Pictorial History of British Achievement

ROBERT WALL

HALSGROVE

First Published in Great Britain in 2000 by Halsgrove

British Library Cataloguing in Publication Data

Data for this publication is available from the British Library

ISBN 1 84114 075 9

HALSGROVE

Halsgrove House
Lower Moor Way
Tiverton
Devon EX16 6SS
Tel: 01884 243242
Fax 01884 243325

Printed and bound in Great Britain by MPG Books Ltd., Bodmin

CONTENTS

To the Memory of

Sir William Reginald Verdon-Smith D.L., Ll.D., F.R.Ae.S.

Chairman of the Bristol Aeroplane Company Ltd
Pro-Chancellor of the University of Bristol (1910 – 1992)

Whose leadership, courage and judgement preserved the
aircraft industry to the benefit of the citizens of Bristol.

INTRODUCTION

In February 2000, the Bristol aircraft industry celebrated ninety years of continuous aircraft manufacture. From small beginnings in a converted bus-shed in the village of Filton, the industry has grown into a large, complicated enterprise which today sustains a major share of the economy of the Bristol region.

The group of factories, design offices and laboratories which line the A38 trunk road on the north side of the city now form the largest aerospace complex in Europe. They make significant contributions in terms of military aircraft, aeroengines and weaponry to the forces of N.A.T.O. and the U.S.A.F., and also supply components to important European airliner projects. The space laboratories of British Aerospace Dynamics Group produce communication satellites which have made intercontinental telecommunication the everyday experience of the ordinary citizen.

Although the name 'Bristol' is no longer carried on the company's products, it enjoyed for many years a singular fame in the aviation world and was applied to some of the best aircraft designs that ever came out of an aircraft factory. Bristol aircraft enjoyed a reputation for rugged reliability, flight safety and quality of build that promoted confidence, particularly among R.A.F. aircrews, who also placed a quite touching faith in the quality of Bristol aeroengines. The present author well recalls how, on joining an R.A.F. station as a newly commissioned and very green engineering officer in 1955, he was immediately accepted in the officers' mess on the simple introduction: 'This is Max – he comes from Bristols'.

The purpose of this book is to tell the story of the Bristol Aeroplane Company and its successor from 1910 to nationalisation and beyond. The city of Bristol has a long history of commercial success, stretching back to pre-Conquest times when the town was founded where a wooden bridge crossed the Avon, creating a safe haven for deep-sea trading on the western seaboard of Europe.

In the intervening centuries the story of Bristol has been the story of her trade. At every stage of her saga, the city merchants have been engaged in the export of manufactured goods and the corresponding import of raw materials such as timber, salt, spices, sugar, spirits, tobacco or cocoa as the demands of the city's industry varied down the centuries.

By the time that the first aviators were taking to the skies in balloons at the end of the eighteenth century, Bristol was firmly established as one of the most prominent commercial centres in world trade. Despite her early contributions to the industrial revolution in the shape of Brunel's railways and steamships, she never quite exploited the new technology of the nineteenth century to the same extent as did the great industrial centres of the North and Midlands, such as Manchester and Birmingham. Indeed her traditional maritime trade was in decline for most of the century and it was in commercial activity based on consumer products such as tobacco and chocolate that her new wealth was founded. To this could be added a sturdy, light engineering trade and, as the century ended, a significant share of the country's tramway and bus industry.

It is not surprising, therefore, that when the aircraft industry came to Bristol it was against a background of industrial strength already developed in another industry, with carefully considered commercial objectives.

Throughout the previous century, Bristolians had a number of opportunities to observe the efforts of those usually penniless pioneer engineers who indulged in the madcap ambition of attempting to build flying machines. One brave spirit had actually made a parachute drop (successfully as it happened) from a balloon over Stokes Croft on the city outskirts before the turn of the eighteenth century. The pioneer, Henry Stringfellow, is said to have used the railways between his home in Chard, Somerset, and Bristol's Temple Meads terminus as a makeshift wind tunnel, thrusting his models through the carriage window of a moving train to observe their behaviour in the resulting slipstream. Much later, in the first decade of the twentieth century, across the Severn at Monmouth, the Hon. Charles Rolls (who had money and therefore should have known better) was making his first balloon flights and setting up his early meetings with Henry Royce which would lead, many years after his death in a flying accident, to his name appearing on the pay packets of thousands of present day Bristolians. Rolls' neglected grave at Llangattock lies scarcely more than 25 miles from the great engine complex at Patchway.

It was in complete contrast to these efforts of the archetype pioneer aviator that the Bristol aircraft factories were founded. Sir George White was already a millionaire with a self-made record of business success when he announced his aviation venture in the spring of 1910. From the first he saw his latest enterprise as a strict business venture from which he would eventually see a healthy return. In the event, he lived just long enough to see his judgement vindicated, having invested at least half a million pounds of his family's money in aviation before his death in 1916.

Since those years, the industry in Bristol has expanded and prospered, although it has had its difficulties and anxious moments along the way. Both world wars caused unprecedented expansion and the company's products grew to include not only aircraft and aeroengines but also armaments, guns, motorcars, prefabricated buildings, plastic components, guided missiles, satellites and ramjets to name a few, while for a number of years it was engaged in the design and manufacture of helicopters.

Around the factories, there grew up in north Bristol a new community which owed its livelihood to the aeroplane. Many families knew no other source of employment and today there are many third generation employees following family tradition in jobs at Filton and Patchway. The ever developing technical expertise required by the industry both in its design and craft skills has led to the creation of new faculties and departments in the universities and colleges of the district which make Bristol one of the most skilled 'high-tech' areas in the world. This in itself has led to significant industrial investment in the city.

In this book the author, himself a 'Bristol' employee for four decades, seeks to pay tribute to those whose foresight, faith, skill, industry and courage have brought the Bristol aircraft industry to the pinnacle of achievement from which it celebrated its ninetieth anniversary. In this task he has been particularly helped by two authors who have gone before – Chris Barnes in his *Bristol Aircraft since 1910*, first published in 1964 and John Pudney's *Bristol Fashion*, written in 1960 to celebrate the Golden Jubilee of the Bristol Aeroplane Company. Much has happened in the succeeding years in the story of Bristol-built aircraft which here is, hopefully, brought up to date. Nevertheless, it is a story without end. Today, as the industry looks towards the twenty-first century, it can do no better than heed the advice of its founder, Sir George White. In his announcement of 1910, he said his objective was to 'give our own city a prominent place in the movement nationally' and to 'take the risks and expense of the endeavour to develop the science from the … manufacturing view'.

Filton, Bristol

Robert Wall

1

'A New and Important Source of Revenue'

1910 – 1914

Sir George White at Bristol – 16 February, 1910

The year 1910 was one of sensational events. Edward VII died, peacemaker and King Emperor, to be succeeded by his son, the modest, sincere and careful George V. In France, a Polish migrant research scientist called Marie Curie isolated a new element. This unfamiliar material possessed strange qualities of radio-activity which would lead to the creation of the atomic bomb and the raging nuclear controversies that presently pre-occupy much of the thinking of modern humanity. It was the year also of the trial of Doctor Crippen and the return of Halley's Comet.

In Bristol, the Great Western Railway was celebrating the seventy-fifth year of successful running, so that only a few people took notice of the arrangements for the Annual Meeting of the Bristol Tramways and Carriage Company. At this routine meeting of shareholders of a prosperous Bristol business, held on 16 February, decisions were about to be announced that would change the destiny of generations of Bristolians. Eventually they would turn the long established maritime city into the aerospace capital of Europe.

Sir George White, Bart., took the chair. A stocky mustachioed figure, in the tradition of Edwardian businessmen, Sir George was already a dominant figure of the Bristol 'establishment'. He was born on 28 March, 1854 of a Bristol family of modest means and educated at the old St Michael's Boys School. Here the headmaster, Ben Wilson, recognised his latent ability and arranged for him to enter the office of John Stanley, a well-known Bristol solicitor. Young White was just thirteen but was put in charge of the firm's extensive collection of law books. It was a wonderful opportunity for self-education and the lad used his time so profitably that, following the passage of the 1869 Bankruptcy Act and the consequent rush of work, George White was put in charge of all Mr Stanley's work on bankrupts – at the age of fifteen! Such precociousness would never be allowed today but White passed on to work on two private measures promoted in Parliament that became the Bristol Tramway Acts of 1872 and 1874. He became an expert on tramway law and was appointed company secretary to the newly-formed Bristol Tramways Company, with a capital of £50,000. He was just twenty.

This might have been enough for most people, but not for George White. The following year he founded his own stockbroking business and was to remain a member of the Bristol Stock Exchange for the rest of his life. He would be, briefly, a member of Bristol City Council (1890-1893) and a J.P. from 1902, but his early life was almost entirely taken up with tramways and stockbroking.

The official portrait of Sir George White, Bart., (1854 – 1916) which hung in the company boardroom in Filton House for many years.

The affairs of the Bristol Tramway Company prospered – the horse-drawn vehicles carried 115,000 passengers in the first month of service – and White had started an industrial and commercial career which was to make him a millionaire, in the days when that soubriquet really meant something. The company experimented with steam traction in 1880 but the vehicles were noisy and inefficient. By 1887, the company had become the familiar Bristol Tramways and Carriage Company and George White was already considering the possibilities of electric traction. In this he was ahead of his time in England. White called back a Bristol engineer, J. Clifton Robinson, from the U.S.A. where electric trams were already operating, and together they opened an electrified line from Old Market Street, Bristol to the Gloucestershire town of Kingswood, in the autumn of 1895. By this time, White claimed that his company had already carried 150,000,000 passengers.

George White next introduced electric tramways in cities as diverse as Middlesbrough, Coventry, Dublin and London. It is not unfair to describe him as the father of the British tram. His foresight and energy brought a complete change in British urban transport and led to the development of prosperous new businesses.

All this allowed George White to practise the good Bristolian habit of philanthropy. He became a Governor of Bristol Grammar School. He erected the Bristol Stock Exchange in St Nicholas Street. When the building was completed in July 1903, it was presented as a gift to his fellow stockbrokers. But it was with his work for local hospitals that George White made his greatest contributions to the welfare of his fellow Bristolians. He was made President and Treasurer of Bristol Royal Infirmary and organised the fund raising that led to the King Edward VII Memorial building. This is another of White's projects that still remains in use today. In 1904, all this business and civic activity led to a well-merited baronetcy.

The Bristol Stock Exchange in St Nicholas Street, built by
Sir George White as a gift to his fellow stockbrokers.

The first headquarters of the Bristol Aeroplane Company at 28 Clare Street
in the heart of Bristol's financial area.

Sir George White was a regular visitor to France. One such visit in the autumn of 1909 led him to take more than a passing interest in the fledgling French aviation business, which was well ahead of the European competition. On his return to Bristol, Sir George took a number of momentous decisions.

When he rose to give his annual report that February day in 1910, there was nothing to indicate that the meeting would be anything but routine. For more than an hour he passed steadily on about financial returns and future investments. It was a short passage just before the end that caused an alert newspaper reporter of the *Times and Mirror* to reach for his pencil.

'May I tell you' said Sir George, 'that for some time past my brother and I have been turning our attention to the subject of aviation which seems to offer promise of development at no distant date. We have determined to develop the science both from the spectacular and the manufacturing point of view. We have determined personally to take the risks and expense of the endeavour to develop the science.'

There is no record of whether the news that the venture was to be funded by the White family personally came as a relief to the assembled shareholders. Certainly Sir George's fellow stockbrokers felt he had gone a little mad and were prepared to say so. But there was more to come.

'I may say' continued Sir George, 'that we have already on order several machines of the best design, with the intention to develop a British industry and to make Bristol its headquarters. If, as we believe, we can make the headquarters close to Bristol, we can give our own city a prominent place in the movement nationally, and secure for the Tramway Company a new important source of revenue, as we shall take care that the centre of attraction is located upon the systems and it is obvious that the public interest in the subject will attract enormous crowds from the whole West of England to witness the numerous demonstrations that will take place.'

Even at this early date, Sir George was referring to aviation as a science. Of the early British pioneers of air transport, Sir George was the only one who saw the whole thing first and last as a calculated business enterprise, operated from the sole view of producing profit. His aim was to build and sell aircraft. If he could fill his tramcars with crowds of sight-seers, then all well and good. Sir George would never be a starry-eyed aviator. Indeed there appears to be no record that he ever flew in an aeroplane. He was, first and foremost, a builder of practical air-machines which performed to specification at a competitive commercial price. In this, only Sir Fredrick Handley Page was any where near his rival. White was undoubtedly the father of British aircraft production.

As the meeting in the Grand Hotel broke up, reaction was mixed. Bristol, for all its vaunted spirit of enterprise, can be incredibly cautious. The idea of flying machines as a staple industrial product was one that its business community found hard to accept. The local press, on the other hand, were enthusiastic and the *Western Daily Press* went so far in its leader the following day to predict 'the time when flying machines will be so perfected that they will be reckoned among accepted methods of travel'.

The *Bristol Times and Mirror* took a more prudent line, careful to shelter in the lee of Sir George's coattails: 'No one can truthfully say after Sir George White's speech that Bristol is lacking in up-to-date enterprise. Sir George is not only abreast of the times, but a little ahead of them.'

This ground-breaking speech was made just a little over six years after the Wright brothers' first flight at Kittyhawk in December 1903. The Wrights had made visits to France in 1908, where they received much more encouraging support than in their own country. By 1909, when Sir George made a visit to a flying display at Pau, the French were leading the aviation scene in Europe, with aviators such as Voisin, the Farman brothers and Blériot making regular and reliable flights. Sir George visited several French manufacturers, among which was the Sociétè Zodiac, makers of the designs of Gabriel Voisin. The Zodiac models had been strongly recommended as containing excellent workmanship and he accordingly acquired the British manufacturing rights.

Three days after the announcement, Sir George White registered four new companies:

The Bristol Aeroplane Company Ltd
The Bristol Aviation Company Ltd
The British and Colonial Aeroplane Company Ltd
The British and Colonial Aviation Company Ltd

If George White was a specialist in anything, that subject was company law, and so he covered all the options of manufacture, transportation and geographical location in his choice of company names. Copyright considerations may also have influenced his choice. Sir George began trading with the third name on the list and a capital of £25,000, a vast sum for those days. The other companies were left dormant with a nominal capital of £100 each, although it was under the banner of the Bristol Aeroplane Company that the venture would see its days of glory.

Sir George White took the chair of the new company, and was joined on the board by his brother Samuel and his son G. Stanley White. Mr Henry White Smith was appointed Secretary and Mr Sidney Smith, General Manager. Both were nephews of Sir George.

The board's first meeting was held on 28 February when the formal agreement with Zodiac was approved and two sheds at Filton were leased from the Tramway Company at its northern terminus in the Gloucestershire village of Filton. All this business was transacted in the company's registered office at 28 Clare Street, the headquarters of Sir George's stockbroking business in the heart of Bristol's commercial quarter. It was all a world away from the rural calm of Filton, which in 1910 was little more than a clump

The tramway shed at Homestead Road, Filton in which aircraft manufacture started in 1910.

Filton House, a family home near the tramway shed, was purchased in 1911 for use as headquarters and offices.

of houses round a small fourteenth-century church and a couple of pubs. Nearby Filton House was still a family residence which the company would buy in the summer of 1911 for offices. The tramway from the city ended near Homestead Road, a side turning off the main Gloucester turn-pike which led to the two galvanised iron sheds which became the first production shop. Off Homestead Road to the right were the new houses of Fairlawn Avenue, built for tramway employees who were required to live 'on-the-job'. Until 1992 Homestead Road was the main entrance to the British Aerospace plant at Filton and the houses in Fairlawn Avenue have long since been demolished after becoming factory offices. But many of them remained as family homes for company employees well into the 1950s.

The original sheds eventually became part of the ultra-modern machine shop complex at Filton. Whereas they began their service to the aircraft industry in an atmosphere of glue, canvas and sawdust, they later housed the numerically-controlled machines which carved intricate aircraft components from solid metal without any apparent human assistance. Together with Filton House, these sheds were still in daily use by the aircraft business, ninety years on from the company's foundation.

The years that followed February 1910 were ones of ceaseless creative activity for the young organisation, which would advance its techniques with a series of new designs which led to the delivery of 260 aircraft from the Bristol factories by the outbreak of war in August 1914. But all this was in the future. The team had yet to assemble and fly its first aircraft, and Sir George was anxious to exhibit at the approaching Air Show at Olympia, due to open on 10 March! So Sidney Smith and another of Sir George's many nephews, Herbert Thomas, were packed off to Paris to study Zodiac production methods and to return with the first Zodiac supplied machine, crated but ready for assembly. The plan was to try out assembly at Filton and then take the machine to the Olympia show. The timescale was tight but just achievable. Following the show, the aircraft would go to the flying ground on the motor race track at Brooklands near Weybridge in Surrey where the company had leased No. 17 Shed for flight trials.

Box-kite assembly in progress inside the tramway shed at Filton in 1911.
The workers employed were largely carpenters and trimmers.

The houses built for tramway workers in Fairlawn Avenue, Filton,
later became the homes of aircraft workers and then offices before demolition in 1989.

In the event, it was providential that the decision was taken to uncrate the aircraft at Filton. The Filton team, now led by newly-appointed Works Manager, George Challenger (son of the Tramways Traffic Manager), soon discovered that the 50 h.p. Darracq engine had no mounting points provided on the airframe. That the said airfame was an exquisite piece of workmanship could not be denied, so special Filton-designed clamps were made and both aircraft and engine packed off to Olympia for the duration of the Air and Motor Boat Show.

After the show, the Zodiac was sent down to Brooklands to Shed 17 for flight testing under the French pilot Edmond, while Challenger and his assistant Collins Pizzey (also of the Tramways) got on with the job of building five more Zodiacs. Sidney Smith was at Weybridge already where he quickly assembled the machine, but it proved consistently under-powered and over-weight and usually refused to leave the ground. Eventually, on 28 May 1910, the Zodiac made a short hop, the sum total of its flying time. The Directors promptly abandoned the Zodiac design and proceeded to law to claim 15,000 francs from the French company for breach of its warranty which guaranteed the ability to fly!

Faced with the failure of the Zodiac, Sir George White now cut his losses in a characteristically hard-headed business fashion. Challenger went ahead with an unabashed pirated copy of the design of a Farman bi-plane and at the same time there were two further important developments. First, Filton got their hands on the new Gnome rotary 50 h.p. engine which was a great advance on the Darracq, and would prove to be the best basic aircraft engine for the next eight years or so. Then, as a development from a failed-bid by Sir George to persuade the British War Office to adopt Bristol aircraft exclusively, there came an agreement to lease a site at Larkhill on Salisbury Plain for a second flying school. This proved a fateful decision. While the Army was traditionally conservative and very reluctant to engage in aeronautics, nevertheless, the early Bristol aircraft did their development flying in the full view of army units based on the Plain and it was inevitable that eventual orders would be placed.

Challenger started building the Farman type bi-planes at Filton in June 1910 and by the end of July, Airframe No. 7 complete with Gnome engine was ready to 'go' at Larkhill. Taxi tests began at 6 a.m. and

Running-up a completed Box-kite on the greensward opposite Fairlawn Avenue. The figure in the long black coat is Sir George White.

The engine and undercarriage installation of a Box-kite.

when Edmond was ready for his first attempt to get airborne, the fateful experience with the Zodiac had its effect on the ground crew. They all went flat on the ground to look for the first minutest chink of light to show between the wheels and the grass strip! This time there was no doubt. The kite-like contrivance, which in itself possessed a certain grace, immediately soared to 150 feet. The Company had a successful design on its hands. The design became known as the famous 'Box-kite' and the Company in due course built 78 of the type. The final batch of five for the Royal Naval Air Service became the first aircraft to be built at the new tramway factory to be opened at Brislington in 1912.

The Box-kite is said to have owed its success to the basic soundness of the Farman design and to the improvements, particularly in producing strong, light structures, that Challenger and his team worked into the airframe. Certainly, when the Farman concern threatened to prosecute the Bristol Company for breach of copyright, the Directors entered a defence of such improvement to the Farman plan as to fundamentally alter the design. The case was dropped.

Throughout the summer of 1910, Box-kites were seen at a number of aviation meetings, including the famous Bournemouth event (where C.S. Rolls was killed) and the first large event in Scotland at Lanark in August. Sir George now argued that aviation was unlikely to proceed at any pace unless there was an adequate supply of pilots to feed the growing demand for both sporting and display flying. While the company would continue with aircraft production, much of its time would be spent on flying training at Brooklands and Larkhill, and the Bristol schools would become the foremost flying venues in the country. As new aircraft were completed at Filton, so they were sent to the flying schools and the available equipment at both venues had been doubled by the time the 1910 season ended. When war broke out in August 1914, the Bristol schools had trained over 300 pilots, 80% of the total then available.

Sir George's other pre-occupation was marketing. Trade missions were prepared for visits to Australia and India at the end of 1910 that showed Sir George's ability to present his company's products in a way that both the public and potential customers would understand.

Even exotic opportunities were considered, and when the explorer Captain R. F. Scott visited Bristol to promote his forthcoming South Polar expedition, Samuel White took the opportunity of a Lord Mayor's reception to offer a Box-kite for the final dash to the Pole. Scott refused – probably wisely.

21 September 1910 saw the first aircraft to operate in British army exercises when a leading British pilot, Capt. Bertram Dickson flew a Box-kite for the benefit of a group of V.I.Ps led by the Home Secretary, Winston Churchill, and including British military notables Kitchener, Roberts and French. It is said by some that Churchill's life-long enthusiasm for aviation started on this day. Five days later, air-to-ground radio communications were first successfully tried out in this country when a primitive spark-and-coherer apparatus was strapped to a Box-kite piloted by the London actor, Lt Robert Loraine. The Larkhill demonstrations led Haldane, the War Minister, to increase the Army estimates for air services from £9000 in 1910, to £50,000 in 1911.

Sixteen Box-kites were built in 1910 and, as the autumn of that momentous year turned to winter, Sir George White's flying schools began to turn out their first certified pilots; the successful pupils receiving the coveted Royal Aero club documents. The first issued at Brooklands was No. 28 to Bristolian Leslie McDonald on 12 November, while a New Zealander Joe Hammond received No. 32 at Larkhill. After this, the army granted permission regularly to its officers to train as pilots if they so wished. But the much canvassed army order for reconnaissance machines seemed to be elusive as ever.

The Filton sheds had by now settled down to a production rate of two Box-kites a month and two French aviators, Maurice Tetard and Henri Jullerot were taken on as full-time test pilots. Engine testing was carried out by the simple device of tethering the tail of the machine to the fence which separated Fairlawn Avenue from the flying ground.

Sir George now judged the time right to introduce the aeroplane to the Bristol public. Accordingly, a temporary canvas hangar was erected on Durdham Down near the Sea Walls and two Box-kites installed. Demonstration flights were given on Friday evening 14 November, by McDonald, but rising winds on the Saturday caused flying to be postponed until the afternoon, when Tetard prepared to take off. By this time the police estimated the crowd to be nearly 30,000 and, as there were no safety barriers, a way had to be cleared for take off. Tetard then took off towards the Sea Walls and, turning down wind to pass over the Avon Gorge, made a spectacular run across the roof tops of Clifton before turning to pass again over the tower of the Downs Reservoir to land safely in front of the cheering crowd. On a later flight, the wind got up to such a degree that airspeed over the Suspension Bridge was – 5 knots! Nevertheless Stanley White and others were taken on flights while, ever watchful for the commercial option, Sir George offered the city's first air tickets at £5 per trip. The first recorded paying passenger was a Mrs Farnall Thurston (a niece of Sir George), who returned to earth breathless and minus her hat. On that windy November day in 1910, Bristolians took the aeroplanes to their hearts. Today the relationship is as close as ever and, over the years, the lives of thousands of Bristol people have been sustained and enriched by the science of aeronautics.

A flight in the Box-kite could be a daunting experience. Pilot and passengers sat in the open on the lower wing, just ahead of the 50 h.p. Gnome rotary engine, which buzzed away like a demented bluebottle. The aviation pioneer Sir Sefton Brancker (who died in the R101 airship disaster) had his first flight in India on a Box-kite behind Jullerot. He described his experience thus: 'The Box-kite is not a particularly comfortable conveyance. The pilot sits on the leading edge of the lower wing with his feet on the rubberbar, while he looks through his knees into space. The observer sits somewhat higher with his legs wrapped round the pilot's body! By the time we had the engine running ... I was thoroughly frightened!'

The main controls consisted of a large joystick which controlled cables from the elevators and ailerons. These hung limp until sufficient forward speed was attained to lift them. Unlike modern ailerons, they worked only in one direction and caused the aircraft to turn but also providing a yaw effect which had to be corrected with a rudder. Rigging was critical to performance and even a minor change of temperature could produce bowed spars, stretched wires and sagging fabric.

An historic photograph of a Box-kite taking off from the Bristol Downs during the demonstration flights organised by Sir George White in November 1910.

Collins Pizzey, Manager of the Bristol Flying School at Larkhill, on a Type T (Improved Box-kite) No. 52 during the Circuit of Britain Race, July 1910.

A Box-kite with pilot and passenger about to take off at Larkhill. Note the rudimentary fairing.

Prier monoplanes under construction in the tramway shed in mid-1911. The foreman's bowler hat was required dress at the time.

Examples of early Bristol attempts to build a monoplane.
The second was a much sturdier machine but neither was successful.

Despite Bristol publicity which claimed that flying a Box-kite was so simple 'that a child could manoeuvre one of these machines in flight', controlling the aircraft appears to have been anything but simple. Years later, two replica machines were built for the film *Those Magnificent Men in Their Flying Machines*. Both survive, one in the flying collection of the Shuttleworth Trust and another on static display in the Bristol City Museum. Pilots who have flown these replicas comment wryly on three characteristics. First, the undercarriage has a nasty habit of breaking in anything up to 50% of all landings, and the film crew soon ran out of spares. Secondly, the machine was unstable in pitch due to a shifting of pressure on the forward elevator, while lateral control was very heavy and the gyro effect of the rotary engine overrode the port aileron's power thus making a left-hand turn well nigh impossible. Drag was also high so that, on engine failure, the Box-kite just stopped dead. Hence getting the nose down was vital if the pilot was to stand any chance of survival after engine failure.

Nevertheless, the all-round view made the Box-kite a first class observation platform and in this lay its sales potential to the military.

So the sales efforts persisted, and in December 1910, using the experience of the canvas hangars gained on the Downs, two sales missions left Filton, one for India under Farnall Thurston with Jullerot as pilot, and another under Sidney Smith for Australia. While much publicity resulted from these trips, there were no substantial sales, although the aircraft was on offer for £1100 complete, of which the engine cost £600 of the total.

The sales break-through had been made, however. On the day that Tetard was thrilling Bristolians on the Downs, Company Secretary, Henry White Smith, reported to his Board that the Russian Government had signed a contract for the supply of eight Box-kites, although the news was to be kept secret for the time being. This success, and other individual sales led on 18 January 1911 to the appointment of Stanley White as Managing Director and an increase in capital to £50,000. Eighty men were now on strength at Filton. Then on 14 March 1911, Secretary of War, Haldane, announced in the House of Commons an order for four Box-kites for the Army, the first British-built machines to be purchased.

If 1910 had been a year of excitement at Filton, the new year of 1911 was equally remarkable for the variety of new designs and for the number of new designers that Sir George and the Board encouraged (and employed) to display their newly acquired skill. The first task was to produce an improved performance over the Box-kite. Monoplane designs appeared easier to build, lighter in weight and with a better turn of speed. While considering these possibilities, Challenger still found time to produce a glider for the newly formed Bristol and West of England Aero Club and to also lay down a production run of six 'Type T' bi-planes, an improved Box-kite which sported an embryo cockpit and, possibly more important, a much stronger landing gear. The Type Ts were entered for several races in the summer of 1911 but a series of accidents, one fatal, led to their disuse after August.

Challenger, meanwhile, had been instructed to set up an experimental department. His No. 2 in this venture was to be Collins Pizzey and both men learnt to fly at Larkhill. Pizzey was so good that he stayed on as Chief Instructor when the heroic Tetard returned to his native France. Pizzey's place was filled by A. R. Low who with Challenger produced the first truly Bristol design, the monoplane of 1911. This little machine, of which two were built, was definitely not a success and defied attempts to coax it into the air. Sir George suspended work on the monoplane and hired a clever Blériot engineer, Pierre Prier, who arrived at Filton to design a series of monoplanes from June until his return to France at the end of the year.

In tandem with the Bristol monoplane, a racing bi-plane was also produced in the early months of 1911. From the board of yet another designer, Robert Grandseigne, this crashed on its first flight at Larkhill in April. Had Sir George realised it at the time, this design could have been a winner because it was the world's first tractor bi-plane, a lay-out which would dominate aircraft patterns for the next three decades.

The second half of 1911 saw three designers operating at Filton and also the arrival of the man who was to become one of aviation's greatest names. First in the field was Pierre Prier who began to prepare a monoplane entry for the prestigious Gordon Bennett Cup Race. The race date was 1 July and Prier was given too little time, so the entry was transferred to the Round Britain Race but Prier himself crashed on the morning of the race. Prier persisted and developed his design to provide a range of two-

*Early Box-kite operations. The officer in the foreground wears a black armband
to mourn the death of King Edward VII who died in 1910.*

The first Prier-designed monoplane outside the sheds at Larkhill in July 1911.

seat machines with which the company set about securing export markets. Particular attention was paid to quality and finish and the series of Prier monoplanes saw the first polished aluminium cowlings and burnished steel components to go into a commercially produced and marketed aeroplane. By the end of the year, Bristol teams under Valentine had clinched sales of Prier two-seaters to the Italian army, and in Spain a demonstration flight before King Alfonso led to orders from Madrid. Howard Pixton took the Prier out to Spain where he was joined by Harry Busteed with Box-kite No. 60. Filton legend has it that Busteed's ability to take the Box-kite aloft from a ploughed field did much to convince the Spanish that Bristol aircraft had something special in the way of rugged construction!

This rear view of a Prier monoplane gives a good impression of the large wing area.

This was not the end of the saga. Pixton went straight from Madrid to Berlin where another Prier was waiting for him to demonstrate to the world's most powerful army and its war lord, Kaiser Wilhelm II. The trip was so successful that a Bristol school was formed at Halberstadt which remained in operation until the outbreak of war. In all 34 Priers were built and examples went as far afield as Bulgaria and Turkey.

While Prier was still at Filton, Eric Gordon England (R.A.C. aviator's certificate No. 68) joined the company as a pilot but soon showed an interest in the engineering side. Challenger allowed him to exercise his talents in a successful conversion of a surplus Type T into a tractor bi-plane. He began a wholly new design for a military bi-plane, the G.E.1 which emerged as a hefty machine using a 50 h.p. Clerget geared down to half propeller revs through a neat chain drive. The crew of two men enjoyed dual control, seated side by side. The machine flew well and Gordon England was asked to develop it as the G.E.2 for the 1912 British military trials at Larkhill in August 1912. Two examples were produced but engine problems, particularly low power output from the Daimler installed in the second machine, led to early withdrawal from the contest, but not before Gordon England had flown for half an hour with his controls lashed tight by his mechanic as a precaution against wind buffeting!

Gordon England left Bristol in early 1913 after producing his G.E.3, a design for Turkey which suffered structural difficulties in the mainspars.

While the efforts of Prier and Gordon England were relatively successful, they did not satisfy Sir George White's search for perfection. He also suffered the first recorded staff poaching in the embryonic industry when Challenger, Low and McDonald deserted to the newly formed Vickers company at Weybridge.

Flying and then dismantling the Gordon England G.E.1 bi-plane at Larkhill in July 1912.

Flying and then dismantling the Gordon England G.E.1 bi-plane at Larkhill in July 1912.

Author's collection

Flying and then dismantling the Gordon England G.E.1 bi-plane at Larkhill in July 1912.

One of the pair of replica Bristol Box-kites built for the film Those Magnificent Men in their Flying Machines.
*One is on static display in the City Museum, Bristol while the other is maintained in flying condition by
the Shuttleworth Trust at Old Worden Airfield in Bedfordshire.*

*Preparing a Bristol-Coanda monoplane (40ft span, 50hp Gnome engine, 73 mph) at Larkhill for the military trials in July 1912.
The two figures with their backs to the camera are Sir George White and his son Stanley. Stanley White (1883–1964)
succeeded to the baronetcy on the death of his father in 1916 and was Managing Director of the Company from 1911 to 1955.*

To continue development of the Prier monoplanes and to fill the gap in the design staff, Sir George recruited a brilliant young Romanian, Henri Coanda, twenty-five years old and son of the country's Minister of War. Coanda was already into ducted fans some twenty-five years ahead of Whittle and brimmed with new ideas. He worked apart from Gordon England on the bi-planes, taking over general responsibility for these when the latter left in early 1913. Gordon England went on to prominence in the motor industry while Coanda remained at Filton until his return to Romania in October 1914.

Coanda's first job at Filton was an up-date of the Prier monoplane, an orthodox two-seater of which six were built, four going to Romania and one to Italy, while the same countries took another six of the the side-by-side version.

All eyes now focussed on the 1912 Military Contests to be held on Salisbury Plain in August and Coanda began work on the design for a military monoplane. Such was the style of things in those days that the War Office issued the rules for the contest on 12 May and expected the complete aircraft to be ready for the air on 15 July. The conditions were strict. The machine had to have good flying capabilities and possess good downward visibility with dual control. It had to fit into a 32ft packing case and also be towed on its own wheels in an army convoy. The pilot had to be capable of starting the engine alone and taking off from a ploughed field if necessary. No wonder Coanda's design was the strongest to come out of Filton to date, with an undercarriage that looked more compatible with agriculture than aviation. It did the job nicely, however, and was the first to be fitted with hand brakes, a useful advance in technology.

Bristol managed to get the Coandas to the trials, serial Nos 105 and 106, flown by Harry Busteed and Howard Paxton, backed up by Valentine. Both aircraft performed well and shared joint third prize of £500 each. The event had its usual share of excitements. On one occasion, Busteed ran into trouble in gusty weather with a high ranking military personage on board as a contest judge. Busteed thought he could solve his problems by landing in a field of corn stooks which would engage the cross spar of his undercarriage and bring him safely to earth. Unfortunately, he reckoned without the engine's propeller which cut all the stook-strings and acted like an aeronautical threshing machine. The aircraft careered across the field spreading a cloud of chaff in its wake and disgorging an irate and highly scared staff officer with his hair full of straw! The Coanda emerged from this incident undamaged.

Readying a Coanda for flight at Larkhill in July 1912. Thirty-six versions of the type were built by Filton and more overseas under licence.

The success gained in the 1912 Military Trials received a severe check the following month. Both Coandas were bought by the War Office and put straight into operation, being readied for the usual autumn manoeuvres. Then, on 12 September 1912, two officers, Hotchkiss and Bellington, were killed when No. 105 crashed near Oxford, it is thought through pilot error, a sharp turn causing the wings to fold. Because this was the latest of the series of (unrelated) monoplane fatalities, the Army immediately banned all flying in any form of monoplane type. Although the ban was lifted after six months, the Oxford accident effectively ended the progress of the Coanda monoplanes, although 34 of all types would be built before production ended in mid-1913. The bulk went overseas to Romania and Italy, although performance was much down-rated by heavy wing strengthening following the accident which killed Gordon England's younger brother Geoffrey on 5 March 1913.

Nevertheless, when Sir George White addressed the annual meeting of Bristol and West of England Aero Club in August 1912 he could already boast that Filton was the largest aircraft factory in the world, working on orders for no fewer than eight different countries. In addition to Larkhill and Brooklands, Julerot was running a flying school in Madrid, while another was in action in Italy. The factory was advertising for apprentices and the office staff was firmly settled in Filton House. Across the city at Brislington, the Tramways Company was expanding its factory and there would be space available here for aircraft production if ever the need arose.

Despite all this activity, the monoplane controversy was a setback. Much of this derived from the success of the B.E.2 bi-plane, designed by Geoffrey de Havilland and built by the Royal Aircraft Factories at Farnborough. Instead of producing its own designs, therefore, Bristol found itself accepting a contract to build the B.E.2a, 19 being included in the first batch. This would lead to a long stay of this aircraft on the production line and the Bristol factories would eventually build over 1000 variants of the type. Characteristically, the workmanship in the Bristol-built version was reputed to be the best in any of the type.

An early version of the B.E.2 at Larkhill. A production order for this Government-designed aeroplane in early 1913 provided the Filton factories with much needed work and the orders were extended well into the war.

Coanda's response to the monoplane ban was to design a bi-plane, the B.R.7, which is said was inspired by the performance of the B.E.2 at Larkhill in August. Employing the same rugged tandem undercarriage, the aircraft was really a Coanda monoplane with an upper plane fitted. It was subjected to fairly rugged structural tests and we find very early examples of structure testing taking place at the National Physical laboratory at Teddington in Middlesex and also at the Eiffel Company's plant in Paris. The engine, a 70 h.p. Renault, was fully cowled and the machine was offered on the market at £1800. Early in 1913, five of these B.R.7s were ordered by Spain following the visit to Filton of a Spanish mission and they were built alongside the first B.E.2s. When the Spaniards took delivery of these machines, they found the performance well below specification and the complete batch was returned. With such commercial disasters, the B.E.2 contract must have been a comforting bread-and-butter source of profit.

The next product from Coanda's drawing board was an unsuccessful seaplane which nearly killed Busteed when its engine overheated and the pilot had to swim for his life in the Solent. The next bi-plane, the T.B.8, was a much better product and 16 in all were built (not 54 as some earlier accounts record). Most of these went to the Royal Naval Air Service and the company used the test site for two seaplane versions at Dale on Milford Haven in September 1913.

As the summer of 1913 progressed, suspicion of German expansionist aims led to the Bristol factory becoming more concerned with war. Further contracts for the ubiquitous B.E.2 were obtained and an agreement was reached with the great Louis Breguet for his factories in France to produce military design under licence. Breguet himself became a consulting designer to the Bristol concern.

Superficially, Filton village did not change a great deal. But there was an active daily scene as workers arrived and departed on the frequent tram services and the buzz of aircraft engines was a constant reminder of the growing factory and airfield that lay behind Fairlawn Avenue and at the foot of Rodney Hill. The aeronautical community had arrived to stay and there was a growing sense among Bristolians that something exciting was happening on their doorstep. There was already a thriving model section of the Bristol and West Aero Club which enjoyed the privilege of testing its model hydroplanes from the lake at Bristol Zoo.

As early as December 1911, Sir George White had set up a secret experimental department at Filton. Located at 4 Fairlawn Avenue it was known as Dept. X. One of the engineers was taken on the payroll as 'Chief Designer'. His name was Frank Sowter Barnwell who came from Scotland to Bristol to create aviation history and a name that remains one of the all-time greats in what his mentor, Sir George White, always described as 'the science' of aeronautics.

Frank Barnwell was born in Lewisham, Kent, in 1880 of a north-country family who sent him to the great Scottish public school Fettes College in Edinburgh. He left at eighteen to serve a six-year apprenticeship in marine engineering (1898-1904) with the Fairfield Shipbuilding Co., of Govan and

Captain Frank Sowter Barnwell (1880–1938) in R.A.F. uniform during the First World War. He joined the Bristol company in 1911 and, with one short break, was Chief Designer and Chief Engineer from 1915 to 1938 when he was killed in an aircraft accident.

Captain Barnwell in the 1930s.

taking a B.Sc. in engineering at the University of Glasgow. After two years with the famous Fore River Corporation of Boston, he returned to this country in 1908 to join his brother Harold in a motor business which he used to support their joint, and much greater, interest in flying. Using their garage at Causewayhead, Stirling, as a base, they produced three machines between 1908 and 1910, the last of which flew quite well. The brothers then came south to sell their skills in the growing aircraft industry. Frank joined Filton in March 1911 while his brother went to Vickers where he became Chief Test Pilot and was killed in an unexplained accident in 1917. Frank was about to go in with A.V. Roe when he got Sir George's much more exciting offer.

So at the age of thirty-one, Frank Barnwell came to Bristol where, with two short breaks, he remained until his untimely death in a flying accident in 1938.

The arrival of Barnwell at Filton marked the first major turn in the Company's history. In these early months of 1911, the Company had two major activities. By far the most profitable was the flying school business which would continue to thrive as part of the Company's activities into the 1950s. At this time it was the Company's primary business, and the purchase of aircraft to sustain the school was a major need. Indeed all the design efforts of Gordon England, Prier and Coanda were concentrated on producing machines which would first and foremost stand up to the treatment they received in the flying school. So successful was the flying school activity that on 30 December 1911, it was announced that the capital of the Bristol and Colonial Aircraft Company would be doubled to £100,000. This was basically to provide new equipment and by this time the Company was offering to train large batches of army and naval officers at very low contract rates. White had grabbed at least half the market in pilot training in the United Kingdom.

Schools were formed in Germany and Spain in 1912 and later that same year a similar school with Bristol money invested opened at Mirafiore in Italy. While they were quite prepared to place their own investment capital on the line, where it was possible to attract local investment in partnership with home based industrialists, the Bristol firm took up any opportunity. Sometimes the attempt succeeded, but on other occasions, as eventually in Germany, the pressures of an expanionist military regime caused Bristol to withdraw. The Bristol money was retrieved from Germany in the nick of time in June 1914. These pioneer years are characterised by a succession of long forgotten but colourful characters. Jullerot and Tetard led the parade, but such names as Hammond, McDonald, Captain H.F. Wood, Maurice Tabuteau, Douglas Graham Gilmour, Captain Dixon, Farnall Thurston and Harry Busteed, deserve to be recorded.

The beginnings of an embryonic production line at Filton can be traced to the order for the B.E.2 which, as we have already seen, was placed in the autumn of 1912. The orders for the B.E.2 meant that Filton received large quantities of drawings prepared in the Government drawing offices. Much of the design work was not up to scratch and considerable time was spent in eliminating snags and bringing the drawings up to the standard that the Bristol factory expected. All this led to the creation of an expert workforce which, as war approached, emerged as the most experienced in Europe. The B.E.2s were ordered in disappointingly small batches and, as even in those days aviation was a constantly improving business, a number of modifications received cut down the rate of production until it was less than profitable. Modifications have always been the bane of the aircraft production engineers' existence and life was no different in 1912. Nevertheless, the B.E.2 provided Filton with useful 'bread-and-butter' orders before and during the war.

The project for which Sir George White engaged the thirty-one year old Frank Barnwell at the end of 1911 was born in the fertile brain of a young naval lieutenant. Charles Dennistoun Burney was the son of Admiral Sir Cecil Burney, one of the leading naval figures of the day. He had been introduced to aviation as a passenger with Howard Pixton in a Box-kite fitted with flotation bags for a flight over Portsmouth harbour in the previous October. Burney saw the possibilities of using aircraft with the fleet. Sir George decided to support him and obtained the consent of the Admiralty to go ahead with experimental work.

Burney's first machine would appear incredible to today's engineers: a bi-plane which floated in the water as a hydroplane with two sets of propulsion, one for the air and the other for the water! This machine never flew, although many experiments were conducted, including a carefully thought out scheme for a pneumatic inflated wing. Barnwell brought much clear thinking to Burney's proposals and cleaned his designs up into a monoplane layout which was eventually tested at the Admiralty base at Dale on Milford Haven in Pembrokeshire during the summer of 1912. All kinds of stability problems were

The Bristol Scout C (span 24ft 7in, 80hp Gnome engine, 93 mph). The original design was sketched by Captain Barnwell in an exercise book for Sir George! The type first flew in February 1914 and over 370 were eventually built for the R.F.C. and R.N.

The Bristol Scout D (24ft 7in span, 100hp Clerget 110 mph). This later version of the Scout was fitted with a spinner and large ailerons.

experienced and when eventually it proved possible to tow the X2, as the craft was named, to anything approaching airspeed, it took off with locked control and the hapless pilot could only sit while the machine plunged back into the water. Fortunately the pilot was unhurt but X2 was a write off.

A further machine, much improved, followed. The weakness of the Burney hydrofoil was the reliance on underwater propellers with all the drag problems that these created. The idea of the simple float plane had yet to catch on but if X3 had been fitted with this equipment she would probably have been a success. The aeroplane was ready for testing in June 1914 but on its first run went aground on a sand bank, sustaining heavy damage. The Admiralty decided that no more funds were available and X3 was brought back to Filton where she was eventually broken up after the First World War. This was the end of Burney's direct partnership with the Bristol Company, but he was to go on to invent the minesweeping paravane, one of the successes of the First World War, also in 'X' Department at Filton, using White family money.

Meanwhile Coanda was continuing his development of the bi-plane. Following the breakdown of an agreement between Bristol and the Italian Government in November 1913, a surplus fuselage came to the attention of Frank Barnwell and he obtained Sir George's permission to drop work on the Burney boats in order to concentrate on a single-seat 'scout' aircraft, a type which was now engaging military attention. Working closely with the pilot Harry Busteed, whose influence on the design was considerable, Barnwell produced the first aeroplane in the world that could be called the forerunner of the classic single-seat fighter. He called it his Baby By-plane and it was a simple little aeroplane of only 22 feet wingspan, using an 80 h.p. Gnome engine. This aircraft was a brilliant exercise in weight saving and together with the pilot and enough fuel for three hours flying, it weighed only 950 pounds. It first flew at Larkhill on 23 February 1914 and was an instant success. Unfortunately, it was lost in a mix up over fuelling during a cross-channel race in July 1914, but by this time Barnwell had two improved versions under construction at Filton. Production of the Bristol Scout came not a moment too soon. A few weeks later, on 4 August 1914, Britain went to war with Germany. The age of the fighting aeroplane was about to dawn.

—◆◆◆—

2

THE WOUNDED SKIES

1914 – 1920

*'To the requisite material of war, Bristol made many contributions,
but perhaps none more important than the constant stream
of aeroplanes which issues from the ancient city.'*

From Charles Wells *Bristol and the Great War.*

Everyone expected the conflict to be shortlived. Frank Barnwell was among the first to volunteer. Some historians have argued that frustration with official policy on aircraft design led Barnwell to join the forces but there is no evidence to suggest that his motives were other than patriotic. He joined the Royal Flying Corps and was commissioned as a Second Lieutenant. Across the city in Fishponds, a rising star of the motor race track and chief designer for the Brazil Straker motor company, the twenty-nine year old Roy Fedden, also attempted to join up. Fedden was turned down because of a football injury. The consequences of this decision of an unknown doctor were to be tremendous, as we shall discover later in this narrative.

The call to the colours left the Filton management with considerable problems. The Bristol flying schools were taken over by the armed forces who became responsible for air crew training throughout the war. In fact, Larkhill had already been closed on 2 June 1914 for manoeuvres by the Royal Flying Corps in collaboration with the Army. All the Larkhill machines and staff were transferred to the Brooklands School which was taken over by the War Office on 17 August. At the outbreak of war 308 out of 664 pilot certificates issued by the Royal Aero Club had been awarded to Bristol students. This supply of trained pilots formed the nucleus of the Royal Flying Corps in 1914.

The dispersal of the schools and the depletion of the Filton staff left Herbert Thomas, the Filton Works Manager, facing the difficulty of stepping up production, while at the same time training replacements, many of them women. Coanda left in October 1914 to return to his native Romania.

*The Bristol Type 6 Twin-Tractor bi-plane (53ft 6in span, 2 x 120hp Beardmore engines, 87 mph) was the first
design that Leslie Frise worked on when he joined Barnwell in 1915. Two specimens were built
but proved to be underpowered and the design was dropped.*

Initial production at Filton concentrated on the B.E.2, obsolete but considered adequate by the War Office. Immediately after the outbreak of war, Filton received an official instruction that nothing but the B.E.2c should be produced. Nevertheless, a further batch of 12 T.B.8s were built and, although ordered for the Army, were delivered in October to the Royal Naval Air Service at Gosport. The T.B.8 proved so satisfactory that the Admiralty ultimately ordered a further 24, all built in the tramway shops at Brislington. They were all delivered by the 24 February 1916.

The T.B.8 was a development of one of Coanda's earlier monoplanes. It was also from one of Coanda's monoplanes that Frank Barnwell developed the Bristol Scout which showed such promising qualities that two improved versions were produced as the Scout B for the Royal Flying Corps, with serial numbers 633 and 634. These two aircraft were probably the best Scouts under construction in any of the warring nations, although across the Channel a Dutchman, Anthony Fokker, was scheming his series of classic fighters for the German army air service. The major drawback in the British industry as the war opened was the complete lack of an indigenous aircraft engine. Britain had the best airframe manufacturers in the world, with Bristol well in the lead, but the reliance on supplies of foreign engines was a major handicap. Nevertheless, the opening months of the war completely changed the commercial prospects of the growing British aircraft business. The war, with its immediate demand for Scouts, was providential for the Bristol Company, just as it was for many others, such as the Short Brothers, Sopwiths and Vickers.

The Royal Flying Corps was well prepared for hostilities and four squadrons were able to cross to France, for reconnaissance activities. The information gleaned in these early forays across the German lines convinced a sceptical General Staff that there might be something in the aeroplane after all. In his first report from France dated 7 September 1914, the Commander-in-chief of the British Expeditionary Force, General Sir John French paid glowing tributes to the work of the R.F.C. These aeroplanes carried no planned armament and the aircrews went aloft armed with rifles or pistols and the grim determination to force their opponents down if they were encountered. From these small beginnings an air warfare strategy began in early attempts to deny the sky over friendly armies to enemy aircraft. On this simple premise rested all the air fighting which developed in France during the First World War. It was largely an affair of Scout aircraft, eventually fitted with machine guns and interrupter gear which allowed guns to fire through the propeller blades and led to a whole string of classic bi-planes. Bristol's contribution was significant. The two Scouts were completed by the end of August 1914 and delivered to the Army at Farnborough. In France their performance earned the praise of the squadron pilots who dubbed them 'Bristol Bullets'. The company received a production order for an improved model, the Scout C, on Guy Fawkes Day 1914. A further two dozen were ordered by the Admiralty. With typical British perverseness the two services now argued about priority on deliveries. The first production Scout C was delivered to the Navy on 16 February 1915. With the Filton factory full of orders for the B.E.2, the Scout was produced at Brislington and the task highlighted the problem faced by the rapidly expanding factory organisation. On the outbreak of war, 200 people were employed at Filton, expanding to 520 by August 1915. The Company introduced a production bonus scheme in June of that year but manpower was always a problem until the introduction of 'reserve occupation' for aircraft fitters at the same time as conscription in mid-1916. The expanding workforce and the arrival of contracts, particularly after the introduction of the Bristol Fighter, demanded for increased space and in September 1916, a large erecting hall was constructed behind the old tramway sheds. This building, expanded again between the wars, is still in use today by the Naval Weapons Division of British Aerospace. In 1916 it represented a vast expansion and alongside it fabric and bolt shops were also built. A Government contribution of £30,000 went into the development of the Erecting Hall (as it was known until the mid-1960s) and a works canteen was built on the old Box-kite test field. Today this forms part of the Works Medical Department.

At Brislington 161 copies of the Scout C and 210 of the improved version, the Scout D, were produced by December 1916. By this time the Scout was hopelessly obsolete but it had pointed the way ahead. None of the Scouts were fitted with formal armament. Indeed, the first two Scout Bs which went to France, went to No. 3 Squadron and to No. 5 Squadron and were armed locally with two rifles for the former and a mixed kit of a rifle, pistol and five grenades for the latter. Some later versions of the Scout D had a fixed Lewis gun on the upper wing and the Naval versions carried explosive darts made by the Ranken company for operations against Zeppelin airships.

Despite the somewhat crude armament arrangements, the Bristol Scout achieved two notable 'firsts' for British aviation. In 1915 a Scout belonging to No. 6 Squadron was fitted with a single-shot Martini carbine mounted on the starboard side in such a way that the bullets missed the propeller. On 25 July, this aircraft flown by the Squadron Commander, Captain Lanoe G. Hawker, was on an evening patrol when he tangled with three German aircraft. Hawker managed to force all three, two Aviatiks and an Albatross, to the ground. He was awarded the first Victoria Cross to be won in aerial combat. The citation read that the award had been made for 'consistent gallantry over a period of time'. Hawker's action in this little Bristol Scout (serial number 1611) must go down as one of the most remarkable aerial flights of this or any war, as the three German machines were all armed with machine guns. The German Airforce had its revenge on the 23 November 1916 when Hawker was shot down by Baron Manfred von Richthofen, while piloting a D.H.2.

The next major feat by the Bristol Scout is unique in British aviation. On the 3 November 1915, one of these versatile aircraft, having been fitted with flotation bags, took off from the very short flying platform of the sea plane carrier H.M.S. *Vindex* and so became the first manned aeroplane fitted with a wheeled undercarriage to take off from the deck of an aircraft carrier. As the *Vindex* had no facilities for landing back on the vessel, the flotation bags would allow the aeroplane to ditch alongside. The pilot was Flight sub-Lieutenant H.F. Towler, R.N., in Scout serial number 1255. The Scout proved popular with the Navy and was used for a number of experiments, including one where a Scout was carried aloft on a three-engined flying boat over Harwich harbour. It was then released at a height of 1000 feet. This experiment was carried out successfully by Scout No. 3028, again from H.M.S. *Vindex*, but the experiment was not repeated. The purpose was to carry interceptor aircraft aloft to deal with Zeppelins but by this time machines were becoming available which could tackle the big airships direct from the ground.

The early months of 1915 saw the arrival on the Western Front of the Fokker E-type monoplane and this brilliant little aeroplane gave Germany command of the sky. It showed up the shortcomings of the B.E.2, which was slaughtered in its dozens, because of poor armament and lack of manoeuvrability. Agitation by the General Staff led to the release of Frank Barnwell from the Army in August 1915. He was sent back to Filton on indefinite, unpaid leave to resume his post of Chief Engineer. From then until the day he died in an aircraft accident in 1938 Barnwell always used his Army rank. Barnwell immediately recruited another engineer whose career was to be equally distinguished. Leslie G. Frise had just graduated from the University of Bristol and joined the Royal Naval Air Service. Barnwell persuaded the Navy to release Frise and he joined the team at Filton, where he would be responsible for very significant advances in aircraft structure and lay the foundations of the designs of most of the Second World War aircraft that came from the factory.

When Barnwell left No. 12 Squadron with its Avro 504s and B.E.2s at Netheravon in August 1915 to return to Filton, he was given the task of sketching two new designs, a single-seat Scout and a two-seat reconnaissance machine. First ideas for the latter machine emerged as a twin-engined aircraft with good durability in order to sustain and see Zeppelin patrols and it emerged in April 1916 as the Twin Tractor bi-plane. By this time, the War Office had established an airfield at Filton on fields at the bottom of Filton Hill alongside the Company's factory and the land already acquired by Sir George White. The TTA bi-plane was flown from this field on the 26 April and another copy on the 27 May. Both were flown by Captain Hooper, the station commander of the War Office Acceptance Park at Filton airfield. Although the machine was tested by the RFC, no production order followed and a scheme to produce a single-engine version foundered. This was probably just as well, because Barnwell by early 1916 was in the thick of producing what proved to be his most outstanding design.

Barnwell's new machine was called R2A. His original design envisaged using a 120 h.p. Beardmore engine and was a twin-seater bi-plane with the pilot in the front seat and the gunner immediately behind him, back to back. The aircraft could fire forward and the gunner gave covering fire to the rear. No sooner had he sketched out the R2A, Barnwell realised the machine was under-powered and he redesigned the layout around a 150 h.p. Hispano-Suiza engine. He had scarcely completed this proposal when the new 190 h.p. Rolls-Royce Falcon engine was produced so the aeroplane was redesigned again, this time with the designation F2A. The letter F indicated that the role of the aeroplane had been changed from reconnaissance to fighter.

The Company obtained an order for two prototypes and the first of these took to the air on 9 September 1916. This machine had considerably improved armament, following a detailed study of the Vickers machine gun by Leslie Frise. This Vickers gun was mounted in front of the pilot, synchronised to fire through the propeller, while a Lewis gun with 360 degree arc of fire was provided for the observer. The type was immediately named the Bristol Fighter and, before it finally went out of service in the 1930s, 5308 varieties of the design would be produced.

The first version of the famous Bristol F2 Fighter (39ft 3in span, Rolls-Royce Falcon III 275hp, 125 mph) which first flew on 9 September 1916. This design by Frank Barnwell founded the Bristol Company's fortunes and over 5308 were built until the type went out of service in the thirties.

The Fighter F2B, production version.

Barnwell realised that he had a winner on his hands and everyone at Filton had awaited the first flight with great excitement. It was all the more disappointing when the pilot, the ubiquitous Captain Hooper, protested that he could not get the aeroplane to fly anything over 6000 feet. Despite several other flights, the magic figure of 6000 could not be passed and in desperation, Barnwell sent for his brother Harold, by now Vickers' Chief Test Pilot. To everyone's consternation, Harold Barnwell also failed to pass the magic 6000 figure although he was certain he had gone much higher. Then the realisation dawned – astonishingly – that the aircraft was fitted with a faulty altimeter. A new instrument was fitted and on the very next flight the F2A climbed to 10,000 ft in fifteen minutes. By this time the Company had received an order for 50 production machines and a line was laid down again at Brislington, as the Filton factory was still churning out its quota of B.E.2s. Barnwell cleaned up the design and improved the wing layout and was rewarded in November by a contract for 200 of the new model F2B. Deliveries began on 20 December 1916 from Brislington and within three months 50 machines had left Bristol. At last the Company had a full production order for a complete Bristol design. Sir George White's vision was beginning to pay off.

It was during the building of the initial batch of Bristol Fighters that the Filton Works received a blow of stunning and desperate suddenness. While writing at his desk at his home, Old Sneed, on 22 November 1916, Sir George White suffered a heart attack and died instantly. Until that day he had been his usual vigorous self, attending a meeting of the council of the Bristol Royal Infirmary that same afternoon.

The grave of Sir George White in the churchyard of St Mary's, Stoke Bishop, Bristol.

Sir George White remains an important historical figure in the industrial history of Great Britain. Curiously, his memory is largely uncelebrated in his native city. It may be that Bristolians are satisfied with the outward signs of Sir George's success in the shape of the Stock Exchange, the Bristol Royal Infirmary, the zoo gardens at Clifton and Hollywood Towers (used to finance the BRI) and especially the great aeronautical engineering factories at Filton. Nevertheless, a prominent monument in the centre of Bristol is still lacking. Essentially a modest man, Sir George would probably prefer it that way, although he would have derived great pleasure from the creation in 1946 of the Sir George White Chair in Aeronautics at the University of Bristol.

His brother Samuel took over as Chairman and his son Stanley, who inherited the baronetcy, became Managing Director. Sir Stanley White was to remain at the head of the company until his retirement as Managing Director in 1955. He remained Deputy Chairman until his death in 1964.

Bristol Fighter production in progress in the Erecting Hall during the First World War. The nearest aircraft already has a Vickers machine gun mounted to fire through the forward fuel tank.

Rear fuselage frames for Bristol Fighters under assembly.

Rolls-Royce Falcon engines being mounted in Bristol Fighters during the First World War at Filton.
The radiator is in position in the machine on the right.

City Museum, Bristol

The First World War. Women played a large part in industry in the Great War
and some are seen here in Filton's mainplane shop.

The First World War. The canteen at Filton laid out for Armistice Day celebrations in November 1918.

Meanwhile production of the Bristol Fighter went ahead at a good pace. Barnwell had completed the aeroplane in conditions of great secrecy. All Filton was in on the secret however and it is remarkable that when the aircraft appeared on the Western Front in the colours of No. 48 Squadron R.F.C. in March 1917, it came as a complete surprise to the Germans. Affairs in the Royal Flying Corps at this time were at a low ebb. The old two-seater aircraft that equipped the corps were completely outclassed by the Albatross DIII which was in general use throughout the German Air Corps. The leading German ace of the day was the legendary Baron von Richthofen, with whom the Bristol Fighter tangled in its very first operation. The R.F.C. staff under Major General Trenchard had decided to allow their pilots to become familiar with the Bristol Fighter and allow numbers to build up before sending it into action. It was not until 5 April 1917 that six Bristol Fighters, led by Captain Leefe Robinson, V.C., confronted the great German ace and his colleagues over the French town of Douai. The British pilots operated the Bristol machines in the orthodox way of a two-seater, manoeuvring the machine to allow the rear gunner to fire. This proved fatal. Four of the Bristols were shot down, two of them by the Baron himself, and Leefe Robinson was taken prisoner. Baron von Richthofen says in his combat report 'we met a new type of British aeroplane which we have not seen before .... we could not recognise its name but our DIII Albatross is, both in speed and rate of climb, undoubtedly superior'.

Four more Fighters were lost on 9 April and seven days later six of No. 48 Squadron's machines ran out of fuel whilst still over enemy lines. Fortunately all but one were burned by their crews to avoid capture. This chapter of losses and accidents got the Bristol Fighter off to a bad start but then, almost by accident, some of the Squadron's pilots began using the machine as an orthodox single-seat fighter. Overnight, the reputation of the Bristol machine was retrieved. Baron von Richthofen soon changed his opinion of the Bristol and by July 1917 over 600 machines were on order. The factory at Filton was again greatly enlarged by an expansion of the Erecting Hall and the Company's first full time test pilot was taken on to the books. Captain Joe Hammond, R.F.C., came to Filton as test pilot in January 1917. By March 1918 orders for 2000 more Bristol fighters had been received.

When the Americans came into the war in April 1917, the Bristol Fighter was among the designs chosen for mass production for their air force. The Americans insisted on using their own Liberty engine and this proved an unhappy marriage with the Bristol aeroplane. It was only after a visit from Captain Barnwell and the decision to use an Hispano-Suzia engine built by Wright under licence that success was obtained. Nevertheless, it was obtained at the loss of the lives of several test pilots, including that of Captain Hammond.

When Hammond died, his successor was Flight Lieutenant Cyril Uwins who joined the Company's staff on secondment from the new Royal Air Force on 25 October 1918. When he left the service in 1919, Uwins joined the Company permanently and flight tested all its prototypes from then until the Bristol Freighter in 1946. He remained with the Company for the rest of his working life and retired as Managing Director.

The success of the Bristol Fighter was founded on its handling capabilities. Once the Western Front pilots were familiar with the machine and had discovered the trick of handling it as a single-seat fighter, they could enter a dog fight and turn almost on equal terms with the best German single-seaters. They also enjoyed protection from the rear using the observer's Lewis gun. This was a significant departure from previous thinking. Many years later, the sole remaining flying example in the United Kingdom of the Fighter, serial number D.8096 was restored to flying condition at Filton and the author was fortunate thus both to work on the aeroplane and also to fly in the observer's cockpit. The observer was supposed to prop himself against a small dickie seat but in effect he remained standing with at least half his body exposed to the elements and the enemy. The test pilots were not allowed to plough it around the sky as they would have wished – to the intense relief of anyone in the observer's cockpit. Although the test pilots found the Fighter rather heavy on the controls and muscle power was needed to fly the machine, it was surprisingly stable and picked up speed very quickly if put into a shallow dive. Fighter pilots always spoke highly of its aerobatic qualities although it was alleged to lose considerable height in recovering from a spin.

The Bristol Fighter was in service with 14 R.A.F. squadrons when the First World War ended and it continued in service throughout the 1920s. Production carried on until 1926, by which time it had been built in ten plants in the United Kingdom and three in America. It remained in service with the Royal Air Force until 1932 and examples were still flying with the Royal New Zealand Air Force as late as 1937. By any standard, it was a wonderful machine.

Designing and creating a prototype using a highly skilled team of engineers is one thing. Mass producing that design using unskilled labour is quite another. When the celebrated Rolls-Royce engineer Claude Johnson, was asked by the Director of the Ministry of Munitions to get small jobbing workshops turning out parts for his engines, he replied that he would rather go to prison because it would produce nothing but 'mountains of scrap'. Johnson was right, of course, but Bristol engineers, in particular the late Frank Davy, produced simple foolproof jigs which allowed unskilled labour to produce accurate components. The Company found that women workers were good at this repetitive jig work and these years of 1917 onwards laid the foundations for a tooling organisation at Bristol whose success persists to this day in the very high technical areas now demanded by aircraft technology. This is the side of the industry which the general public seldom sees but all the startling displays of aircraft at aeronautical shows rest on the patient technology of the designer and production engineer. Quality mass production was learnt at Filton in the years of the First World War and has never been forgotten. Again, the technique of off-loading work to sub-contractors has to be mastered. Orders have to be placed on time, materials obtained and supplied, the quality of sub contractors' factories checked and their supply of components to programme insisted upon.

Tinsmiths at work on components for the Bristol Fighter.

The Bristol Company supplied a complete airframe to each sub-contractor as a sample together with all the templates required to produce the ribs and frames and detailed drawings of all jigs and tools required. It established the family practice for such forms of sub-contracting and its example was copied by many other manufacturers both in Great Britain and in the United States.

While the main war-time effort of the Filton factory was the production of the Bristol Fighter, other machines and designs continued to appear from Barnwell's drawing board. Contemporary with the Bristol Fighter was the monoplane Scout, the MIA, built as a private venture. Monoplanes remained unpopular with the Chiefs of Staff and it is possible that Barnwell conceived the machine following the success of the Fokker E1, the layout of which the Bristol machine closely resembled. When the MIA was ready for its flight on 14 July 1916 in the hands of Fred Raynham, it was found to be astonishingly fast for its time, achieving 132 m.p.h. Raynham was so exhilarated that he proceeded to fly under the Clifton Suspension Bridge. Just before Sir George White died, he had negotiated the sale of the MIA to the army and had received an order for four similar machines. Although the aeroplane went into production in mid-1917

Forging ahead 1. The attractive fighter monoplane, Bristol MIA (30ft 9in span, 110hp Clerget, 132 mph) which first flew on 14 July 1916. 130 of the type were built but were relegated to the Middle East front for operations against the Turks. A version sold to Chile carried out the first Trans-Andean flight on 12 December 1918.

The Bristol Type 25 Braemar II heavy bomber (81ft 8in span, 4 x 400hp Liberty, 125 mph) was first flown by Captain Uwins on 18 February 1919. The Braemars (two built) were Bristol's first effort at a large aeroplane but the end of the World War meant that no production order was placed.

for 125 copies, it was never used on the Western Front. Instead it was sent out to the Middle East where it was wasted in dealing with the limited Turkish Air Force. Six MICs were exported to Chile and one of these found lasting fame on 12 December 1918 when it made the first flight across the Andes from Santiago in Chile to Mendoza in Argentina and back.

The production of the B.E.2 aeroplane was phased out in 1917 and the Ministry of Munitions proposed that it should be replaced with a programme to build 50 flying boats of the Porte F.3 type. Bristol would be responsible for the project overall and also build the wing and tail and then assemble hulls built elsewhere. The project foreshadowed exactly the way in which Concorde and Airbus airframes would be assembled but the idea was somewhat advanced for 1918. The cost of transporting the machines to the coast proved uneconomic and so the scheme was dropped.

Bristol's second excursion into large multi-engined aeroplanes proved much more interesting and successful although production orders did not result. This was the huge Braemar tri-plane, designed by Captain Barnwell to meet the need for a very large bomber with the range to penetrate deep into Germany. The design led also to its civilian equivalent the Pullman, a large passenger liner and the Tramp, an equally large freighter. Judged on appearance and looks, the Braemar is the most remarkable machine to come out of Filton. Its three huge wings towered above the runway. These large tri-planes appeared to be the logical way to go in design trends in 1918 and other designers used the type as well, particularly in Italy. It must be said that Barnwell's design was probably the most successful of the tri-planes although it never went into production. In other parts of the world, tri-planes suffered ferocious accidents, largely due to the combined effect of unstable structures and unacceptable aerodynamic drag.

After Barnwell had been wooed away from his first idea of a central engine room for four engines driving the propellers through geared links, W. T. Reid produced a reasonably orthodox machine using four engines in tandem pairs. There was nowhere at Filton large enough to build such a monster under cover and so the machine was laid out in one of the War Office hangars at the foot of Filton Hill. Even

The Bristol Type 26 Pullman tri-plane airliner for 14 passengers was a civil version of the Braemar using same dimensions and power plants, which flew in May 1920. The enclosed cockpit was an unpopular innovation with pilots who carried fireaxes for escape. Only one of the type was built. Two examples of a freighter version called the Tramp were built in 1922 but never flown.

Forging ahead 2. The Bristol Type M.R.I. fighter (42ft 2in span, 180hp Wolseley Viper, 110 mph) was the first all-metal aircraft built in Britain and when it came out in October 1917 was well ahead of its time. Two were built, the first with wooden wings and this machine crashed in the hands of Captain Barnwell at Farnborough on 19 April 1919. He was unhurt.

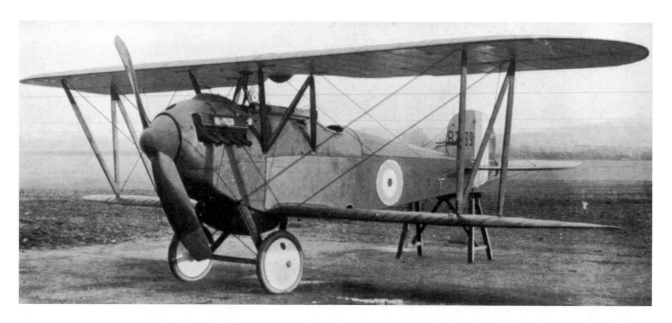

The Bristol Type 21 Scout F (29ft 7in span, 200hp Sunbeam Arab, 138 mph) was the first Bristol prototype to be test flown by Captain C.F. Uwins. This was on 4 September 1918. Uwins was at the stick for most first flights until 1946. The end of the war precluded any production order for the type and only four were built.

so, the wings could not be put on inside and the whole contraption had to be wheeled out sideways and finally assembled in the open air. All was ready in August 1918 and Fred Raynham flew the Braemar successfully on the 13th of that month. Later the huge machine flew to Martlesham Heath and it was later based at Farnborough. The end of the war spelt the end of the project but the Company pressed on with the civil version, the Pullman, which first flew in May 1920.

The Pullman had a uniquely high standard of passenger cabin, something that would not reappear until the 1930s. The crew were in an enclosed cockpit in exactly the same fashion as today's airliners. Pilots were not very happy with this because in the event of a crash they would be unable to escape and always carried firemen's axes when flying the machine.

For the freighter version of the Braemar, the so called Tramp, the Bristol team returned to the idea of a central engine room driving the airscrews through geared shafts. Two prototypes were built and assembled at Farnborough but difficulties with the transmission system kept both aircraft firmly on the ground.

Other projects of the war years were the new single-seat fighter, the Scout F, another two-seater, the Badger and an interesting all-metal version of the Bristol Fighter.

By the beginning of 1918 the Company's workforce at Filton and Brislington had expanded to over 3000 people. It had also seen the first trade union branch formed and when the first Works Committee formed in March 1917, its membership was remarkable for the diverse nature of the unions represented. Each department in the factory elected one of its shop stewards to act on the Works Committee and this form of constitution has persisted with very little variation, to the present day. Now one would

The Bristol Type 23 Badger II twin-seat fighter (36ft 9in span, 400hp Cosmos-Jupiter 1, 142 mph) was the first aircraft of the many powered by Fedden and Butler's classic 9 cylinder Jupiter. The first flight was 24 May 1919 in the hands of Uwins. The direct drive Jupiter, Engine No. 1 was fitted.

City Museum, Bristol

The Parnall Panther fleet reconnaissance bi-plane (29ft 6in span, 230hp Bentley BR2, 108 mph) under construction at the Coliseum works, Park Row, Bristol in 1919. A large production order was cancelled following the 1918 armistice and the Bristol Aeroplane Company finished off those machines in progress.
The central fuselage was hinged for stowage on ships and it can be clearly seen.

Mrs M. Stamper

The Parnall Plover single-seat fighter (29ft span, 436hp Bristol Jupiter IV, 142 mph) was the penultimate design to come out of the Coliseum works and first flew in 1923. A production batch of ten served on the carrier H.M.S. Argus, the only R.N. carrier in commission at the time.

expect to find the Amalgamated Society of Engineers (as it was then), the Woodworkers and the Sheet Metal Workers represented. But it is somewhat surprising that Ernest Bevin's Dockers Union also appears on the Filton Committee. In 1917 there were nine women representatives, all unmarried! The first chairman of the Works Committee was A. J. Bickell and he was succeeded in 1918 by T. J. Skottow. For the duration of the war there were very few disputes of a serious nature at Filton and only four short strikes. The early trade union documentation at Filton that survives shows a sturdy independence and every sign of that determination on the one hand to develop high skills while not allowing anyone however important to push them around. There is every indication that when the Works Committee was first formed, the Company management refused to recognise it. However recognition was eventually won and, to quote from a union news sheet of the time 'a better spirit was created throughout the work and that various causes of unrest and irritation soon began to disappear'. No doubt morale in the factory was also boosted by a visit from King George V and Queen Mary who visited Filton on 8 November 1917 to see the Bristol Fighter in production.

While the main aeronautical activity in Bristol during the First World War was concentrated at Filton, there were other centres of activity. The acceptance part from which eventually the R.A.F. station Filton emerged not only accepted and tested aircraft produced at Filton but was also used for the formation of Royal Air Force squadrons. At Filton a squadron would receive its equipment and carry out its familiarisation with its aeroplanes before leaving for the Western Front or further airfields in the United Kingdom. Ten R.A.F. squadrons were formed at Filton during the First World War and the airfield has kept a link with the Royal Air Force ever since its foundation. We shall see later the foundation of 501 Squadron R.A.F. and its link with Filton and Bristol, continued by the University of Bristol Air Squadron which was based at Filton until 1992.

Another feature of Bristol's wartime aeronautical industry is to be found in the Brazil Straker car factory at Fishponds. Here the young Roy Fedden was Chief Designer, and trying his hand at improving Curtis engines supplied to the Royal Navy for use in the famous 'Jenny' aeroplane. The Fishponds factory was taken over by the Admiralty in January 1915 and switched completely to war production. It was the only factory that Rolls-Royce would trust with the manufacture of their engines and, in particular, large numbers of Falcon power-plants were produced for the Bristol Fighter. This work made Fedden a well known figure at Filton and probably initiated the train of events which led him to join Bristol in 1920.

The other aircraft concern operating in the Bristol area during the First World War was Parnall & Sons which began life in Broadmead manufacturing weighing machines. Parnall eventually became part of the W. & T. Avery Group of Birmingham and from a date early in 1915 undertook the building of sea planes for the Admiralty. Parnall utilised a number of factories for this work. The first was at Myvart Street, Eastville and there were other buildings on Feeder Road, in Redcross Street and also at the Company's earlier building in Broadmead. Incredibly, the Coliseum, a skating rink on Park Row, was acquired for use as an assembly hall.

Harold Bolas was appointed Chief Designer and Andrew Murray Works Manager, while George Parnall himself acted as General Manager. Production began with the manufacture of 150 Short- designed sea planes and a number of Hamble Baby manned planes for training use in Royal Naval flying schools. Seventy-four of these conversions were assembled using the sea-plane version of the Baby as a prototype. The firm then obtained a large contract to produce the Avro 504 which was to become the standard training machine for the Royal Air Force. Parnalls produced both the type B and the type C and then later the famous type K which flew on as an R.A.F. trainer almost until the Second World War.

Simultaneously with their production work, Parnalls began to develop aircraft of their own under the leadership of Bolas. This they did in an experimental shop at Brislington, using a flying field at Yate for their air tests. Their Panther two-seat reconnaissance aircraft was the first British machine specifically for use from aircraft carriers. A hump-backed, ugly looking aeroplane, it was nevertheless a successful design. The purpose of the hump back was to give the pilot and observer a good forward view for landing on carriers, even though entry to the cockpit was through a hole in the top wing. Parnalls secured an order for 300 Panthers but this was reduced to 150 with the end of the war in November 1918. The construction was taken over by the Bristol Company and completed at Filton during 1919 and 1920. The Panther remained in service with the Fleet Air Arm until 1926. Parnalls produced 1000 aeroplanes during the First World War but so diverse was their activity that they also produced

11,000,000 bedsteads, 100,000 bomb crates, 8000 hand-grenade boxes and a host of useful items such as huts, shelters, tables, cupboards and powder boxes. As the war ended, Bolas had also commenced work on the Parnall Plover. Again, this was a naval aeroplane designed as a single-seat carrier fighter and capable of rapid conversion from a land plane to an amphibian. The aeroplane appeared to have great potential but only about a dozen were built.

Aviation had fully established itself as a major Bristol industry when the armistice was declared on 11 November 1918. The Board at Filton immediately granted three days' holiday for all employees. When the celebrations were over, the euphoria was replaced by a grim realisation that times were about to change drastically. All overtime was cancelled from 14 November and on the 26th the Company received formal notice ending all existing contracts for aircraft and spares. Peace had returned – with a vengeance.

3

FLYING BY ITSELF

1920 – 1930

'For the future, the British civil aviation business must fly by itself'

Winston S. Churchill, Secretary of State for Air at The Guildhall – 13 October 1920.

In the autumn of 1920, Winston Churchill was Air Minister in Lloyd George's Government. He had carried the blame for the Gallipoli fiasco, and had returned to the Cabinet to preside over British aviation at a time when the fledgling industry faced some of its worst years. On 13 October Churchill called together the leaders of the industry for a conference in London's Guildhall and Henry White Smith attended, taking Frank Barnwell with him. White Smith was under no illusions about the difficulties facing commercial aeroplane builders in the immediate wake of the World War.

Whilst Captain Barnwell restricted himself to a straightforward technical paper on aircraft structures, Henry White Smith went right to the heart of the matter, pointing out the scarcity of orders, the large surplus of the military equipment and the difficulties of obtaining finance for the purchase of materials. Churchill's response was characteristic, although it did not reflect entirely his lifelong enthusiasm for aviation. In a speech to the conference dinner he made it very clear that British aviation would have to 'fly by itself'.

Churchill's stark message to the industry came as no surprise to the Bristol Board. As early as December 1918 the Company renegotiated the cancellation of the Bristol Fighter contracts and the Air Ministry agreed to accept and pay for all the aircraft already in production, nearly 800 machines at Filton and 192 at the Brislington works. Filton also took over the Panther contract from Parnalls. Large-scale redundancies in the 3000 strong workforce were avoided but it needed all the ingenuity and commercial skill of Herbert Thomas to fill the factory with non-aviation work. Barnwell, meanwhile, was asked to review the design situation. The Board were looking for changes and perhaps did not get all they wanted from Barnwell. His immediate project was for a conversion of the Bristol Fighter into a small cabin machine called the Tourer, and many of the Directors' ideas were centred on flying boats, particularly for services to South America. These ideas originated in an enquiry from the Royal Mail Line, who were looking at ways of speeding up the mail services to Rio de Janeiro and on to Buenos Aires. It seems ludicrous today that serious consideration should have been given to steam propulsion and internal engine rooms but the steamship company had many trained steam-engine engineers on its books and these would need to be found employment! The project culminated in the Tramp freighter but the transmission systems from the central engine room to the propellers out on the wings proved recalcitrant and the type never flew.

Barnwell had a number of other projects under way including the Bristol Babe and the Badger Fighter and consequently there was a viable programme of aircraft for the next two or three years. Thomas obtained much of the alternative work from the motor industry, with coach building contracts for the Bristol Tramways Company. Armstrong Siddeley Motors also placed substantial orders for car bodies and the Company even did some experimental but ultimately unprofitable work of its own on a small motor car.

The year 1920 proved a significant turning point in the story of the City's industry. Three separate events, were to have a profound impact. The first was an order from the Air Ministry for more Bristol Fighters. After the conclusion of hostilities in 1918, the Royal Air Force found itself with a vast surplus of aircraft, a Government that was retrenching rapidly and very few modern aircraft designs on the drawing board. There was a strong school of support for all-metal construction but the money required to develop metal structures was not forthcoming. In October 1920 the Air Council decided to adopt a general purpose type of machine which could serve in a variety of roles. It was to be capable of operating as a single seater or to carry an observer and the specifications required all-metal construction. This was in line with Barnwell's and

*The Bristol Type 28 Tourer (39ft 5in span, 230hp Siddeley Puma, 117 mph) was one of a series
of converted F2Bs prepared for the civil market in 1919. 33 in all were built.*

*Barnwell designed the Type 30 Babe (19ft 8 in span, 45hp Viale, 85 mph) for the private
pilot market but, even after up-powering to a 60hp Rhone, only three examples were ever built.*

Frise's general thinking but as a stopgap, the Bristol Fighter was put into production again as the Royal Air Force's main army support weapon. This order, with repair and renovation contracts, kept the aircraft side of the business going at Filton during the lean years of the 1920s.

The second significant development in 1920 was the 'in-house' transfer of the assets of the Company from the British and Colonial Aeroplane Company to the Bristol Aeroplane Company, the flag under which it would achieve its greatest fame. The prosaic reason for the change was the avoidance of Excess Profits Duty following the World War and the Company's tax advisers argued that it would be far more advantageous to discontinue the existing business and transfer the assets to a new trading company. So the Bristol Aeroplane Company Limited came into existence on 6 March 1920 with a share capital of £1 million, a startling rise from the £100 share capital on which the old company had traded. Very few companies in modern British industrial history can claim such a record of expansion as the British and Colonial Aeroplane Company. From ten employees in a converted shed in 1910 it had expanded into the largest aircraft factory in the United Kingdom, covering 8 acres.

The third development was by far the most significant. We have already referred to the collaboration that went on in 1917 between Barnwell and the Straker Brazil factory at Fishponds which produced Rolls -Royce engines for Barnwell's Bristol Fighter. Straker Brazil's Chief Engineer, Roy Fedden, was now to enter the Bristol aircraft scene and to remain one of its dominant figures for the next twenty-three years.

Alfred Hubert Roy Fedden was born on 6 June 1885, the third son of Henry and Mary Elizabeth Fedden, a prominent local family of sugar refiners who lived on the outskirts of the City in the village of Stoke Bishop. While Roy was still young the family moved to Henbury and it was here in an old Quaker meeting house called 'Fern Hill' that Roy Fedden grew up. At Clifton College, he developed a lifelong love of sport and played on the opposite side in the historic cricket match in 1899 when A.E.J. Collins made 628 not out, the highest all time record innings in the history of the game.

Henry Fedden intended that his son should join the Royal Navy. However, the young Roy failed to pass the Admiralty medical examination and was no more successful in trying to get into the Royal Marines. He was offered a place at Sandhurst, but had already realised that service life was not for him. The Fedden family were among the first in Bristol to purchase a motor car – it was registered AE4, the fourth in the City; Sir George White had AE10 – a Panhard still owned by the family. Here was something that he instinctively understood and loved and it took him only a short time to realise that engineering must be his chosen profession. The decision came as a profound shock to his parents. Engineering was hardly the career for boys of good families, but they did not stand in the young man's way. In September 1904 Roy became an apprentice with the Bristol Motorcar Company, working there by day and studying at night at the Merchant Venturers Technical College.

At the Bristol Motorcar Company's works in Redcross Street, Roy Fedden got his grounding in practical engineering – how to run a lathe, use a drill press and all the techniques of hand forging, fitting, grinding and heat treatment. He added the theory of engineering under Professor William Morgan at the Technical College and by the time his three-year apprenticeship was closing, he had designed his own small motor car. Armed with the drawings, he approached the managing director of the Fishponds-based motor manufacturers, J.P. Brazil.

Brazil took to the young Fedden. More importantly he saw in the car design an attractive commercial proposition and invited the young man to join his staff as junior draughtsman. In the car's first year of production, about 150 were made and sold and Fedden became Chief Engineer of Brazil Straker at the age of twenty-two. He became a well known figure in the British motorcar industry and spent considerable time racing his own Company's product. The Straker Squire cars sold well up to the outbreak of war in 1914, by which time Fedden was the Company's Technical Director. The Fishponds factory grew to over 2000 workers turning out cars and lorries for the army. This continued until January 1915 when the entire factory was taken over by the Admiralty and required to produce new Rolls-Royce aero-engines. Fedden could now use his small design team on aircraft engines. Soon his factory was building the 6-cylinder Rolls-Royce Hawk and then followed up with the Falcon vee 12, the redoubtable power plant for the Bristol Fighter. These water-cooled in-line engines were now taking over from the air-cooled rotaries which had powered most allied aircraft. The water-cooled engines were more powerful and rugged, but the air-cooled engine still had its supporters. So, when in 1917 the Admiralty called for a new design of engine, laying down strict control on size and weight but looking for 30 h.p., Fedden and his team decided to submit a design. The result was the Mercury engine, a 14-cylinder radial which was turned out in the remarkably short time of five and a half months. An order for 200 copies followed. Nevertheless, the Mercury was not altogether successful and Fedden decided to go ahead with a larger and better engine. This basic design for a 500h.p. 9-cylinder air-cooled radial, which he called the Jupiter, would be the most important aircraft engine of the 1920s. Its great advantage was that it weighed just over 660 lbs.

The Jupiter attracted the attention of the Air Ministry but as engineering success arrived, so commercial success began to slip away from the Straker Brazil Group. Brazil himself joined the Imperial Tobacco Company and the Fishponds works were bought up by an international conglomerate called Cosmos. Fedden was allowed to carry on as Technical Director at Fishponds. As the war ended, he turned his attention once again to the motorcar business. In 1919, Cosmos sold off the car side of their empire but allowed Fedden to keep the aero-engine development going. Interest in the Mercury and Jupiter came from a number of quarters. Henry Royce attempted to recruit Fedden into his own company, an offer which Fedden refused. Across the City at Filton Captain Barnwell was looking for an engine to power his new Scout Type F after the failure of the Sunbeam Arab engine. The Mercury fitted the Scout well and the third prototype took to the air on 6 September 1918, the first of the Fedden engines to fly.

The second aircraft to receive the Fedden designed Cosmos Jupiter I was the Sopwith Schneider Trophy entrant for the first post-war contest at Bournemouth on 10 September 1919. Thick fog forced the cancellation of the event but the aircraft was probably the fastest entrant. This was the only Bristol-built engine to power a Schneider Trophy entrant.

The Jupiter also got into the air in a Bristol prototype. Barnwell fitted it in the second of his three Badger two-seat fighters and the machine took to the air, with Captain Uwins at the controls, on 24 May 1919. Another Jupiter engine was used by the 1919 Schneider Trophy team but, although the Jupiter-powered sea-plane was undoubtedly the fastest machine entered, the event had to be cancelled due to the dense sea mists off Bournemouth.

Fedden in the meanwhile, was also producing a light engine called the Lucifer, using an Avro 504K as his flying test bed. Then the roof fell in. Brought down by reckless trading in Russia, Cosmos went into liquidation and the Bristol factory including Fedden and his team was on the market. The Official Receiver allowed Fedden to continue his development work while an anxious Air Ministry looked around for a prospective buyer. Armstrong Siddeley and Vickers demurred but Captain Barnwell's knowledge of Fedden's engines and of the man himself led him to argue to the Board of the Bristol Aeroplane Company at Filton House that here was a valuable asset they ought to acquire.

Driving probably the hardest but the most successful bargain in the whole of the Company's history to date, the Board bought Fedden, his design team, the good-will of the business and all drawings and tools together with five Jupiter engines and 50 sets of raw material for £60,000. The deal was a finely balanced one. The cost had not been prohibitive but, at the same time, if the experiment was unsuccessful, Henry White Smith was heard to remark 'we must cut our losses and get out of engines'.

Fedden persuaded the Company to purchase some redundant R.A.F. buildings at the village of Patchway, and the new engineering department was established there on 29 July 1920.

The White family, meanwhile, was wrestling at Filton with the effects of the economic depression. In 1920 Bristol would produce fewer than 200 aeroplanes – about 10% of the previous year's output – but the search for innovation went on apace. A new wind tunnel had been opened in June 1919 and this, coupled with the arrival of the Mercury and Jupiter engines led to some interesting new designs. We have already seen that the first Jupiter engine to fly went aloft in the Bristol Type 23, the Badger two-seat fighter. Only three Badgers were built but its wings were used for the so called Badger 'X', a sports bi-plane using the Badger's wings and tail surfaces. Work was also proceeding on the Babe, a very small light bi-plane and the civil version of the Bristol Freighter, the Bristol Tourer. The Babe was an attempt to enter the private market but in the event only three were built.

A.H.R. Fedden (1885-1973, later Sir Roy Fedden) with L.F.G. 'Bunny' Butler and the Cosmos team that he brought to Bristol when the Engine Division was founded on 29 July 1920. Fedden is in the centre of the front row and Butler is on his left. The photograph dates from 1931.

The nine-cylinder Jupiter engine with which Fedden sustained the Bristol Company throughout the twenties and early thirties. This is the 520hp Mark VI which powered many classic British and foreign aircraft and was the most popular power plant of its time.

Fedden was in early touch with Barnwell even before he joined Bristol. The Bristol Type 32 Bullet (31ft 2in span, 450hp Cosmos Jupiter 1, 155 mph) was designed to Fedden's request and first flew on 24 July 1920. It was used for air racing in the next three years and led eventually to the Bulldog.

The other Bristol design flying in 1920 was the Bullet, not to be confused with the nickname given to the Bristol Scout in 1914. Roy Fedden was looking for a test bed for his new Jupiter engine and particularly with the object of high speed manoeuvres in mind. Consequently, Barnwell designed an aeroplane of great strength and the completed machine went on exhibition at the Paris Show in December 1919. Although the Bullet flew in the Kings Cup Air Races of 1920, '21 and '22, its main role was to support the third Badger in getting a type clearance for the Jupiter engine, now a Bristol product. The speed was eventually worked up to 145 m.p.h. by which time the Jupiter had been uprated. In its final form the Bullet was expected to achieve 175 m.p.h. but the Company withdrew from racing after the 1922 event.

But none of this activity led to a production order. Barnwell grew disheartened and in September 1921 resigned to take up a technical commission in the Royal Australian Air Force. He was succeeded as Chief Designer by Wilfred Reid. Reid had been working on a new design for a 10-seat airliner and the prototype had already flown successfully in the hands, again, of Captain Uwins on 21 June 1921. The 10-seater was a successful aeroplane. The first was powered by a Napier engine but the other three aircraft built all received the Jupiter. The Bristol 10-seater was the equal of any machine produced at the time. The first copy, powered by a Napier engine, eventually was sold to Instone Air Services. The second 10-seater was fitted with one of Fedden's new Jupiter engines in the spring of 1922 and the performance improved considerably. The machine did not get an air worthiness certificate, however, until July 1924 when the Jupiter Mark IV engine had passed its type test. By that time Instone Air Services had been merged into the new national airline, Imperial Airways Limited, which was receiving a Government subsidy.

The Bristol Type 53 Bullfinch (38ft 5in span, 450hp Bristol Jupiter 1, 137 mph) was a single-seat monoplane all-metal fighter which was developed into a twin-seat sesquiplane. Three were built but no production order followed.

The second 10-seater therefore became a freighter but its performance was to have a significant effect on Imperial Airways' policy. The airline decided that its future aircraft should be fitted with Jupiter engines and this made a considerable improvement in the fortunes of the Bristol engine factory.

Reid and Fedden collaborated on other projects using Jupiter engines, following Barnwell's departure to Australia. Among these were the Bristol Racer, a machine somewhat ahead of its time with a retractable undercarriage and a streamlined engine, a version of the Bristol Fighter fitted with a Jupiter engine and early sketches for the Bloodhound two-seat fighter. Other projects using Fedden's smaller engine, the Lucifer included the M.I.D. racing monoplane and the light aircraft, the so-called Taxiplane.

While he schemed his engines, Fedden's remarkable mind ranged over all the possibilities of future aircraft propulsion for Great Britain. His investigations covered fuelling, materials, mechanical operation of valve gear and he spent a great deal of time looking at the training of engineers. It was Fedden, right at the outset, who persuaded Sir Stanley White of the need for an apprenticeship scheme for the training of future craftsmen. It says much for Fedden's foresight and for Sir Stanley's careful backing of him that the basis of the Bristol companies was laid during these years.

The first achievement of the new engine department came in September 1921 when the Jupiter II passed the Air Ministry Type Test and was the first air-cooled engine to do so. By this time nearly £200,000 had been spent and the Board was getting worried. The breakthrough came at the Paris Air Show of 1921. A very large contract was signed with the French company Gnome-Rhone to build the Jupiter under licence. By the end of 1921 foreign interest in the Jupiter was considerable and testing proceeded both in England and France throughout 1922. The engine eventually emerged triumphant when, following a hard bargain driven by Sir Henry White Smith with the Air Ministry, the Jupiter was officially adopted by the R.A.F. An order was placed in September 1923 for 81 Jupiter IV engines. This gave the department the basis it needed for future expansion.

*The Bristol Type 62 10-seater (54ft 3in, 450hp Napier Lion, 122 mph) first flew on
21 June 1921 as a medium-sized airliner. It was so successful that it was bought by the
Air Council for commercial service. It was used by Instone on London-Paris services
and by Handley Page on London-Cologne.*

*The second 10-seater was powered by a 425hp Jupiter IV and had a modified undercarriage.
It was used by Imperial Airways for freight work and did much to impress the airline
as to the advantages of the Jupiter as a power plant for their fleet.*

*The Bristol Type 79 Brandon (54ft 1 in, 425hp Jupiter IV, 115 mph) was developed as an air
ambulance from the 10-seater design. First flown on 19 March 1924 by
Captain Uwins, it served in the R.A.F., stationed at Halton.*

Rolls-Royce

The Bristol Cherub 1 light aircraft engine 32hp which Fedden and Butler developed in 1923. All drawings by the duo had the prefix FB, as seen on the crankcase of this engine.

The Bristol Type 83 Primary Trainer (31ft 1in span, 120hp Bristol Lucifer, 96 mph) formed the basic equipment of the Reserve Flying School which was in operation by July 1923. Twenty-four of the type were built for various customers and survived until 1933.

The Bristol Type 72 Racer (25ft 2in span, 510hp Jupiter IV, 220 mph estimated) first flew in July 1922 and was the first Bristol machine to have a retractable undercarriage. In flight the aircraft developed many problems, and after seven difficult sorties and many mods, the type was abandoned.

At this time, Fedden's closest co-operator was L.F.G. 'Bunny' Butler. Butler had the task of translating Fedden's schemes into the hundreds of detailed drawings needed to produce a modern aircraft engine. The initials of both men preceded the part number of every Bristol engine, so a Bristol part was easily identified as F.B.1234. The first R.A.F. aircraft to fly with a Jupiter was a Gloucester Night Hawk and the type was also specified for the R.A.F.'s new fighter, the Hawker Woodcock. The success of the Jupiter coincided with Barnwell's return from Australia. Over the previous two years Fedden had co-operated with Wilfred Reid. Of the types which the two men produced, the type 72 racer was the most amazing machine. It was literally a Jupiter with a small aeroplane tacked on behind and it quickly proved that the airframe was not strong enough for the power of the engine. On two occasions Uwins nearly lost his life when the wings twisted to such an extent that complete reversal of control was obtained.

In 1923, Barnwell unashamedly pleaded to be taken back, a request that was acceded to readily. With Barnwell's return, the Bristol Company now had one of the most formidable teams that the aircraft industry had seen in this or any other country. Fedden's insatiable drive continually improved the Jupiter until it would be built in 17 foreign countries and sell a total of more than 7100 engines, to be fitted in over 260 different types of aircraft. Barnwell had more experience of aircraft structures than most British and foreign designers and he also possessed a first-class deputy in Leslie Frise, while Harry Pollard was beginning to make a name for himself in aircraft development. As Chief Test Pilot Cyril Uwins had acquired more experience in the previous three years than most pilots in the business. His careful handling of aircraft and patient courage in difficult situations were the ideal foil for the steel of Fedden and Barnwell. These three would continue at the head of the Company's activities on the aeronautical side until Barnwell's untimely death in 1938.

Much has been written about the relationship between the engineers and the Board of what was still a family company. It has been alleged that Fedden considered the Board autocratic and remote, and lacking in understanding of engineering. No such view appears to have been expressed by Barnwell or Uwins, yet it is interesting that only the latter ever made it to be a full director of the Company and eventually becoming Chairman. Fedden was never made a director, although this was not unusual for the time. On the other hand, the Board had good reason to suspect the cost control aspects of Fedden's work. In the event Fedden remained Chief Engineer there for twenty-three years and it is difficult to believe that the Board was 'autocratic and remote' for that entire period.

For the remainder of the decade, Fedden's activities at Patchway concentrated both on developing the Jupiter and introducing a number of new engines. The Jupiter raced through Mark V, VI, VII and VIII by 1928, each Mark with additional improvements. By the time the Mark IX came in early 1929 the engine was producing 525 h.p., that is well over twice the power available from the first Jupiter produced by Cosmos. The Jupiter probably found its apotheosis in the Jupiter XFBM which was fitted in the great Handley Page HP42 airliner of 1929, using Bristol-patented gas starting procedures operated from the cockpit of the aeroplane.

Other engines produced by Fedden in the 1920s were the small flat twin Cherub of 1924, the Orion, a development of the Jupiter VI in 1926 and the Mercury a significant engine which again was a Jupiter development. Other designs were the Titan of 1927 and the Neptune of 1929. As the decade ended, Fedden was already looking ahead to a larger engine giving at least 800 h.p. and one of the most famous Bristol engines of all time, the Pegasus, was beginning to take shape in his mind. All this, coupled with research into diesel aeroplane engines and a persistent interest in the sleeve valve, came from the genius of this remarkable man as the 1920s turned into the 1930s.

Barnwell and Frise now turned their attention to a series of Bristol designs, all of which were based on the same construction principles. Pollard had developed high tensile steel strip construction while he was working in the Midlands and this type of structure would be standard in Bristol aeroplanes until the arrival of light alloy in the early 1930s. Pictures of Bristol aircraft of the day before they received their fabric cover show a remarkable tracery of light but very strong structure, coupled with workmanship of the highest finish and quality. All the remaining aircraft of the 1920s were powered by Bristol engines and ran through a series of titles all beginning with the usual Bristol 'B'.

Barnwell settled down to produce a version of the Bristol Fighter powered by Jupiter engines. This greatly improved the performance of the Fighter but it was not adopted by the R.A.F., and the designer's first new design after his return suffered the same fate. This was the Berkeley bomber, the last Bristol design for a decade to use other than a Bristol engine. There then followed the Brownie, the

The Bristol Type 84 Bloodhound (40ft 4in span, 436hp Jupiter V, 130 mph) bi-plane fighter shown here in the form used for endurance trials of the Jupiter VI between Filton and Croydon, from January to March 1926, logging 25,074 miles without engine servicing. The pilots Captains Minchin and Barnard, appear in the photo.

The Type 76 Jupiter Fighter (39ft 3in span, 425 Jupiter IV, 134 mph) was an attempt to up-date the F2B with the powerful Jupiter engine. It first flew in June 1923 but orders for only 12 training versions were obtained, some for the Filton Flying School.

Bristol's second attempt at a bomber design, the Type 90 Berkeley (57ft 11in span, 650hp Rolls-Royce Condor III, 120 mph) first flew on 5 March 1925 but, after satisfactory trials, was rejected as unsuitable for night bombing. Three specimens were built.

The Bristol Type 91 Brownie light aircraft (30ft 7in span, 33hp Bristol Cherub, 70 mph) was a response to an Air Ministry competition for light aircraft and first flown by Uwins on 6 August 1924, then later the same day by Barnwell. Three were built but proved expensive to maintain and operate, being no match for the de Havilland Moth.

The Bristol Type 93 Boarhound two-seat fighter (44ft 9in span, 425hp Jupiter VI, 142 mph) was first flown on 8 June 1925 and is best remembered for the initial use of rolled metal section developed by H.J. Pollard.

The Type 93A Beaver was an uprated version of the Bloodhound but equally unsuccessful in the market.

*The pretty little Bristol Type 99 Badminton Racer (24ft 1in span, 450hp Jupiter VI, 160 mph)
which first flew on 5 May 1926 but was lost in a crash on 26 July 1927 at Winterbourne, when
the engine seized. The pilot, Captain F. Barnard, was killed.*

*The Bristol Type 101 Twin Seat Fighter (33ft 7in span, 450hp Jupiter VI, 160 mph) was the penultimate
design of a series of fighter aircraft produced by Barnwell at Filton during the twenties. It first flew
on 5 August 1927 with Uwins at the controls. It did not get a production order but was used for
racing and as a testbed. Fitted with a Mercury II, it broke up in mid-air on 29 November 1929.*

The Type 95 Bagshot twin-engined night fighter (70ft span, 2 x 450 Jupiter VI, 125 mph) possessed a semi-cantilever wing which proved flexible in flight and provided several hair-raising flights before the type was grounded. Sir Archibald Russell was an early flight observer on Bagshot and his memoirs are highly entertaining.

The Bulldog enjoyed international success and became the standard fighter for eight airforces. Here Chief Test Pilot Captain Cyril Uwins (second left) entertains a Latvian delegation at Filton. Uwins was Chief Test Pilot until 1947, Assistant Managing Director, 1947-57 and Deputy Chairman 1957-64.

Rolls-Royce

Fedden and his team steadily developed the Jupiter through the twenties and the super-charged Mark VII of 1928 proved an ideal power unit for the highly successful Bristol Bulldog. By 1930 the Jupiter was the principal power unit of over half the world's air forces and airlines. It was fitted to 262 different types of aeroplane.

Bulldogs of No. 3 Squadron performing aerobatics at the RAF Show at Hendon in July 1935.
This display was for years the annual highlight of the show.

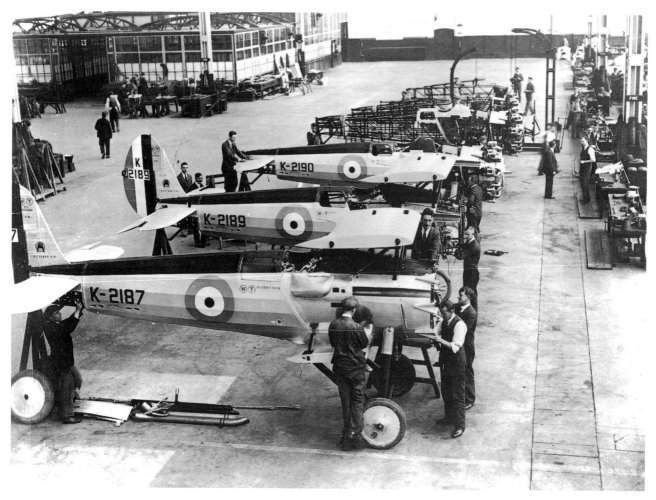

The Bulldog assembly line in the Erecting Hall in 1931. 441 Bulldogs in all were assembled there.

*The line continues! The preserved Bulldog and a BAC Lightning formate in the colours of No. 56 Squadron in 1962.
Front fuselages for Lightning Mk Vs were assembled at Filton. Bristol Chief Test Pilot Godfrey Auty in Bulldog K2227
flies with Squadron Leader John Rogers over R.A.F. Coltishall on 17 September 1961.*

The Bristol Type 107 (30ft span, 450hp Jupiter V, 190 mph) was a lightweight version of the Bulldog which flew in April 1928 but was not ordered into production.

The Bristol Type 109 Long Range bi-plane (51ft 2in span, 480 hp Jupiter VIII, 90 mph) which was capable of 5000 miles range but its heavy load at take-off limited the airfields it could use.

Boarhound, the Beaver, the Bagshot and the Bulldog. There were also Bristol types 109, 110A, 118 and 120. With the exception of the Brownie, a light aircraft using Fedden's Cherub engine and the Bagshot, a monstrous monoplane fighter which suffered from structural instability in the wings, all these aircraft were bi-planes built in high tensile steel structures. The only exceptions were the Badminton and the Type 101 which were of the old type wooden construction. The designs were a rolling development which culminated on 17 May 1927 when the Bristol Bulldog prototype made its first flight in the safe hands once again of Captain Uwins. By 1927, R.A.F. staff thinking on fighter aircraft had gone through several stages. France was considered to be the only potential enemy of the day, and that country possessed a large but relatively slow bombing fleet. Thinking on fighter design changed from very fast machines powered by Rolls-Royce in-line engines to a light fighter powered by air-cooled engines. It was in response to the latter specification, issued as F.9/26 that Barnwell schemed the first ideas for the Bulldog. Originally he had requested the Mercury engine from Fedden but as this was taking longer in development than forecast, Barnwell eventually specified the Jupiter. It was actually with the Jupiter that the Bulldog went into production for the Royal Air Force. The machine handled well although all Bulldogs were very heavy on the controls and it required care in landing and take off. It could be very vicious in response to elevator mishandling and all pilots were very careful while operating near the ground. There were some spectacular accidents, notably that in which Sir Douglas Bader, then a junior R.A.F. pilot, lost his legs in 1932.

The Bulldog made its first public appearance at the Royal Air Force Show at Hendon in July 1927 and soon became a familiar sight after the Bulldog II, an improved version which flew in January 1928, went into production at Filton. The Company had already produced under sub-contract a batch of Armstrong Whitworth Siskins, but the Bulldog contract was the only major production order received at Filton during the 1920s. An initial contract for 25 machines was followed by further orders and the Erecting Hall at Filton was busy with two parallel production lines. The Bulldog was used widely in the R.A.F., equipping no fewer than 10 squadrons and remaining in service until 1937. All told the R.A.F. bought 312 Bulldogs and many others were exported to the air forces of Australia, Denmark, Estonia, Finland, Latvia, Siam and Sweden.

Arrangements were made with the Japanese Government for the Bulldog to be built under licence by the Nakajima Company in Tokyo. Two prototypes were built and assembled, using a Japanese-built Jupiter. However the Japanese Government did not proceed with the order although many original Bristol ideas eventually turned up in Nakajima aircraft during the Second World War!

The Bulldog is best remembered for the astonishing R.A.F. acrobatic displays at Hendon and other aircraft shows before the Second World War. It was incredibly manoeuvrable and the sight of these little silver bi-planes in their colourful markings carrying out all kinds of co-ordinated manoeuvres thrilled the crowds. The Bulldog was not used in action by the R.A.F. but it gave a very good account of itself when used by the Finnish Air Force against the Russians in the winter war of 1939 - 1940. It was a joy to work on. The present author assisted in restoring the Company's original demonstrator aircraft. A team of fitters under Ron Brown got the aeroplane back to flying condition, after we had scoured redundant aircraft stores nationwide. The restored aeroplane flew at Filton Air Day in July 1961 in the hands of Ian Williamson, one of the Company's test pilots and put up a tremendous display. Unfortunately this last example of a flying Bulldog was destroyed in a crash in the 1960s.

Bulldog production kept the Filton factory occupied well into the 1930s. This was just as well, as American designers were already into stress skin construction and the days of the large bi-planes and the little manoeuvrable fighters were numbered. In Germany, Adolf Hitler was already getting mass support for his vision of a new Germany, heavily armed and embarking on the road to military glory. To those who could take the warning, which included Fedden at a very early stage, Britain would need to look to her armaments.

Before turning to the 1930s and the period of re-armament, two other aspects of Bristol aviation of the '20s must be recorded.

As the 1920s opened, the Parnall concern was still operating in the Bristol Coliseum in Park Row, where it was liaising with Filton on the construction of 150 Parnall Panther carrier-borne aircraft. These Panthers were used on board the two Fleet Air Arm carriers *Argus* and *Hermes*. The Panther was the pioneer of modern deck landing and, despite accidents and a Bentley engine that required constant servicing, it was a significant aircraft in the history of naval aviation and deserves a place in the record books.

While the Panther was being produced Parnall and Bolas were working on the Puffin, a single float amphibian. They announced a new version of this machine on 7 September 1921 but were unsuccessful in obtaining production orders. With the loss of the Panther production contract, the Birmingham company of W. & T. Avery withdrew from the Parnall concern and George Parnall carried on alone. He retained Harold Bolas as Chief Designer and the first design from the new company was another naval aircraft, the Plover, a single-seat bi-plane fighter. Of three prototypes, one used an Armstrong Siddeley Jaguar engine while the other two used Bristol Jupiters. The Plover was intended to double as a land plane and twin float sea plane but it proved inferior to its main competitor, the Fairy Fly Catcher, and only 12 Plovers were built. It was an attractive looking aeroplane and deserved a better fate.

Parnall went on in 1923 to produce the Possum, a weird three-seat tri-plane with a Napier Lion engine buried in the fuselage driving the air screws on the wings through a shaft transmission. The shafts themselves were buried in the wing sections. The Possum was intended to be a fast airmail machine according to the Air Ministry who commissioned it. It had a span of 46ft but suffered from mechanical problems with the engine drive. It remained an experimental machine although one of the two samples built is alleged to have flown in June 1923.

John Cleverdon

*Rear view of the Parnall Possum. The second prototype was the last Bristol built
Parnall aircraft before the company's move to Yate in 1925.*

In the same year Parnall produced a single-seat light aeroplane, the Pixie, which took part in the Lympe Air Races on 11 October. It was very similar in appearance to the Bristol Brownie but used a 500 cc Douglas motor cycle engine. Four Pixies were completed, two of them as bi-planes which were later converted into monoplanes. These latter aircraft used the Bristol Cherub engine.

Parnalls persisted in the '20s with naval aircraft and in 1926 produced two prototypes of the Pike, a Napier engine bi-plane capable of amphibious operation: the Perch, another amphibian and the Peto, which was a remarkable little aeroplane. The Peto was a small sea plane built to operate from the Navy's large M2 submarine for which a hangar was provided on the vessel's deck, with a launching catapult. The aeroplane was built of stainless steel to avoid corrosion from the sea atmosphere. Two prototypes were built and the aeroplane actually operated from the submarine.

The project ended when the M2 was lost off Weymouth, possibly due to water entering the hull through the opening of the hangar doors. The final Parnall design of the '30s was the Pippet, a new naval fighter using a Rolls-Royce XII engine. This was not adopted by the Navy leading Parnalls to undertake sub-contract work for other companies.

After creating two light aircraft called the Elf and the Imp, Bolas produced his last design for Parnall, the Pawn of 1930, a single-seat flying boat built for the Air Ministry. This was the smallest British flying boat ever produced with a span of only 28 feet 5 inches. Bolas then emigrated to America and was succeeded as Chief Designer by H.B. Dark. By this time Parnalls had relocated to Yate, where the successor factory still exists.

The Bristol and Wessex Aeroplane Club was founded in 1927 by such enterprising spirits as Captain R. A. Hall and Havergal Downs-Shaw. They had the support of Cyril Uwins, Chief Test Pilot of the Bristol Aeroplane Company and already a figure of some standing in British aviation.

George Parnall offered the club facilities at his airfield at Yate but they decided, probably with the encouragement of Uwins, to go to the nearer aerodrome at Filton. At this time the Air Ministry promoted aviation by subsiding flying clubs with the aim of creating a national reserve of pilots in case of emergency. As the Club developed, it soon became clear that Filton was becoming a seriously overcrowded airfield. The Bulldog production line at Filton was in full swing and there were also many experimental machines under test. Then there were the R.A.F. Volunteer Reserve machines of 501 Squadron, in addition to the Flying Club's Moths. It became clear that some action would have to be taken and it was here that the directors of the Flying Club used their contacts with the City Council.

The City Council resolved to seek a site for a municipal airport and a search carried out on its behalf revealed two farms in Whitchurch, south of the City: Filwood Farm and Tynings Farm with nearly 200 acres.

Landing areas of 1000 yards in an east to west direction and 800 yards north and south, allowed the largest aircraft then in service such as the Armstrong, Whitworth Argosy or the HP42 to operate from the field.

An air rally at Bristol Airport soon after it opened at Whitchurch in 1931. The Hawker Audaxes of 501 Squadron are at top left and a variety of DH Moths dominate the civil air park.

City of Bristol

At its meeting on Tuesday, 9 November 1929, the City Council appointed a committee to look after all its aeronautical affairs. That committee has been known ever since as the Airport Committee. A full licence for the new airfield was received from the Air Ministry on 7 February 1930 and by that time the construction of a hangar and also a club house for the Bristol and Wessex Flying Club had commenced.

Bristol Airport was officially opened on Saturday, 31 May 1930 during a two-day aviation meeting. The opening was performed by His Royal Highness Prince George who would later become the Duke of Kent and die on active service during the Second World War. Prince George arrived at Filton by air in the morning, using a Westland Wapiti Army Co-operation machine in which he flew quite frequently. This was powered by the well tried Bristol Jupiter and before coming to Whitchurch, the Prince visited the Westland factory at Yeovil to inspect Wapiti production. During the ceremony it rained unceasingly, but this did not deter a crowd of 30,000 people staying on to watch the air pageant which followed. The Duke and other dignitaries made speeches and then there was a full acrobatic display, including the R.A.F. Display Team using Bristol Bulldogs. It has been rumoured that Amy Johnson, the famous long distance flier of the time was present. What is certain is that Will Hay the well known comedian was a popular visitor. Among the aircraft present was the flagship of Air France (or Air Union as the French flagcarrier was then known). This was the 12-passenger Liore et Obivier 'Golden Ray'.

Bristol now had its airport and the City Council gave over the responsibility for operating it to the Bristol and Wessex Aeroplane Club. The first Airport Manager was Flight Lieutenant L.E. Winters who also doubled as Secretary of the Aeroplane Club. This arrangement of the secretaryship of the club being held by the Manager of the Airport was to last until well after the Second World War. In the early years of its development, Whitchurch Airport was used almost exclusively by the Bristol and Wessex Aeroplane Club and by visiting private aircraft. In July 1930 it was a staging point for Kings Cup Air Race and Bristol had to wait until 11 July 1932 when the first paying scheduled passenger service set out from Whitchurch. The Chairman of the Airport Committee, Alderman Senington, became the first passenger in a trial Bristol-Cardiff airline pioneered by the British Air Navigation Company Limited. The aeroplane concerned was the well tried Fokker 7. Insufficient passengers were forthcoming and the service ended in a few weeks. Later on, Bristol Air Taxis, run by Norman Edgar who had an aircraft sales business at Whitchurch, operated a De Havilland Fox Moth on the Cardiff route and in 1933 he was able to form Western Airways and run a small service between Bristol-Cardiff and Bournemouth, using a De Havilland Dragon.

In 1933 the Airport Committe added a new hangar and also a tarmac apron to the small field. The extension from the Airport to Airport Road was completed in that year, giving the Airport a main access into the City Centre.

In all, the new airport gave Bristol aviation a brave start to the thirties.

—◆—

4

PEGASUS RISING

1930 – 1939

On the morning of 16 August 1930, anyone watching the skies to the north of Bristol would have seen one of the most beautiful and spectacular sights ever created by aeronautical engineers. His Majesty's Airship RI00 was returning from a triumphant two-way crossing of the Atlantic and a visit to Canada. As the giant airship passed to the north of Bristol on its way to its home base at Cardington in Bedfordshire, the aircraft of No. 501 Squadron R.A.F. took off from Filton to escort the giant vessel on her way. It was one of the most dramatic moments in Bristol aviation. The RI00 was returning to a Britain suffering from the effects of the world-wide economic depression and with unemployment rising rapidly towards the three million mark. Despite the economic gloom most British manufacturers had a number of new designs in preparation, as did engine producers. Very few would ever get into production but the building of prototypes and the developing of those into production machines usually took several years. Together with repair and maintenance work, this development work kept most factories going and Bristol was no exception. The reserve flying school at Filton continued to be active and therefore the Company kept very much in the mainstream of British aviation activity.

No. 1 Machine Shop at the Engine Division works at Patchway in the early thirties.

Rolls-Royce

Bristol Mercuries under assembly at Patchway in the thirties.

The airfield, flying school (left) and engine shops between the wars.
R.A.F. Filton hangars can be seen at the top of the picture.

1930 saw new personalities at the helm of the Bristol Aeroplane Company and new developments in aviation in the Bristol region. The establishment of a Royal Air Force Reserve squadron at Filton was among the most important. The Royal Air Force Reserve was founded to provide the full-time Air Force with what was in fact a territorial organisation. The theory was that qualified pilots could serve the squadron in their spare time and a number of these units were established near the great cities of the United Kingdom. No. 501 Squadron, the unit allocated to the City of Bristol, was formed as a bomber squadron and dates from 14 June 1929. It started life operating elderly Avro 504 Ms and these were followed with De Havilland DH9As in March 1930. It began to re-equip with the Westland Wapiti in September and soon became a fully equipped unit. The Air Ministry had been developing a special version of the Wapiti for the reserve squadrons and No. 501 received the first of these, the Westland Wallace in January 1933.

No. 501 Squadron was based at Filton up to and beyond the outbreak of war. The year 1936 saw massive expansion. The R.A.F. Reserve became the Royal Auxiliary Air Force and 501 Squadron renamed 'County of Gloucester' to increase the recruiting area. There were new aircraft in the shape of the Hawker Hart, replaced by the more modern Hind at the end of December 1938. In March 1939, No. 501 Squadron received its first modern fighter, the Hawker Hurricane and every weekend these machines could be seen around Bristol as the pilots strove to achieve operational status. When war broke out in September 1939 the Squadron took part in the air defence of Bristol but then left the City for Tangmere and an exciting wartime career.

By the time the 1930s opened the Bristol Aeroplane Company was under the leadership of a new Chairman. Mr. Samuel White, the brother of Sir George had continued as Chairman of the Company with Sir Stanley White as Managing Director until 1928. Sir Henry White Smith had left the Company after a disagreement in 1925 and Sir Stanley would remain Managing Director until well after the Second World War. Another member of the family, Sir George White's nephew, was Mr William Verdon-Smith. William Verdon-Smith had spent his early career as a stockbroker and had gained great expertise in company law and commercial practice which led to his appointment as Secretary of London United Tramways in 1901. From here he went on to become Managing Director of Bristol Tramways and maintained a life-long interest in transport in all forms. He joined the Board of the Bristol Aeroplane Company Limited in 1927 and the following year took over from Samuel White as Chairman. William Verdon-Smith would be Chairman for the next twenty-seven years and preside over the affairs of the Company during its greatest years.

1930 was the eleventh year of Fedden's service with the Bristol Aeroplane Company. He had made the Jupiter the greatest aircraft engine in the world, producing a fortune for his employers. Apart from many air forces around the world, the British national airline Imperial Airways relied almost entirely on the Jupiter for its big lumbering airliners. In particular the Handley Page 42s, so much the trade mark of the British airliner of the '30s, performed faultlessly on the Jupiter and in May 1931 the airline introduced three Short flying boats, the Kent Class, also relying on the Jupiter for power. Later two big land-plane versions of the Kent, the Short Scylla and Syrinx were introduced and spent their time on the London-Paris route until the outbreak of war. By this time most of the Imperial Airways Jupiters had been running for 10,000 hours each with great reliability, showing how right Fedden was in his insistence on good basic design, careful development and meticulous maintenance.

Even the Jupiter could not go on for ever and Fedden's ever active mind looked at several improvements in the early 1930s. It was from his Mercury that the first Pegasus was developed. Originally the Mercury V but with many improvements, in particular enclosed valve gear driven by two push rods and with automatic fuel and oil control systems for rapid take off from cold, the Pegasus was an instant success. It first ran in 1932 and by 1936 had been developed to produce over 800 h.p., rising by 1939 to over 1000 h.p. for a weight of 1110 lbs.

One of Fedden's preoccupations was with propellers. The day of the old wooden fixed-propeller was ending and in the United States variable-pitch airscrews were under development. This meant that the propeller could be set fine for take off and then adjusted later for cruising. Fedden could not persuade any British manufacturer to put the money up front to produce such a propeller so he began development at Patchway to produce propellers of his own. These were fixed-blade propellers but demonstrated how Fedden's mind was working. Meanwhile production of the Pegasus went ahead and by the time it ended in 1943 17,000 'Peggies' had been completed. The Mercury ran in parallel with the Pegasus at Patchway and with 21,993 engines. That exceeded even the 'Peggy's' production figures.

City of Bristol

The 546hp Bristol Pegasus I of 1932 was the first aero-engine over Mount Everest and went on to power a range of aircraft, including WWII veterans like the Stirling and the Sunderland.

A sectioned Pegasus preserved in Bristol Industrial Museum.

Rolls-Royce

The ubiquitous Bristol Jupiter was used by aircraft firms world-wide but few more strange than the installation of twelve Siemens licence-built Jupiters of 'push-pull' capability installed in the giant Dornier Do X flying boat. The craft was hard pushed to make 1000ft of height.

The engine company was keeping the Bristol Aeroplane organisation very much in the front of the development race. The supply of reliable engines was critical and engine development in those days took much longer than the production of an airframe. It is one of history's happier accidents that Fedden's development of Pegasus and the Mercury happened to coincide with the rise to power of Hitler in Germany and the realisation that Europe could not be very far from a world war.

The first years of the 1930s were lean ones for the aircraft division at Filton. When production of the Bulldog came to an end, the factory was not to receive another one in such numbers until the Blenheim I went into production in late 1935, following an ITP – the industry jargon for 'Instructions to proceed' – for the detailed drawings for 150 machines to Air Ministry specification 28/35. In the intervening years, only 17 Bristol serial numbers were issued and of these, only 14 were built, 11 getting into the air. Nevertheless, there were some interesting designs produced. The Type 109 long range bi-plane of 1928 was Barnwell's next product after the Bulldog. It was a private venture intended to break long-distance records and was planned with a range of 3300 miles. However, the aeroplane never left Great Britain and was broken up in 1931 but not before it had done some useful development flying with the later marks of the Jupiter. Two examples of the next design, the Type 110A, were built to house Fedden's medium range engine, the 5-cylinder Titan of 250 h.p. which he conceived for small passenger aircraft. Many components used in the Bulldog appeared in the Type 110A and by the time the design was sufficiently developed to start construction of a prototype, Fedden had gone on from the Titan design to a slightly larger engine, the Neptune, going up from five to seven cylinders and using many common parts with the Jupiter. These joint efforts show that, no matter what Fedden's relationships were with the Board, he had a close working partnership with his fellow chief designer. The 110A first flew on 21 October 1929 using a Titan and early in 1930 the Neptune replaced the smaller engine. The project came to an end, unfortunately, when in February Uwins ran the aircraft on to a rough part of the airfield, the undercarriage failed and came through the fuselage floor, just missing the test pilot. The machine was not rebuilt.

The Filton Inspection Department in the late thirties.

The IIOA was followed by the Types 118 and 120 bi-planes, which were unashamed private ventures derived from the Company's success with the Bulldog. The objective was to break into the lucrative market for army co-operation machines which had been brilliantly exploited by Westland with the Wapiti, followed by Fairey with the Gordon. The design of the Type 118 coincided with the adoption of the Mercury V as the Pegasus by the Air Ministry in late 1930. The first prototype flew on 22 January 1931 and proved a very versatile aircraft, carrying out the role of fighter, bomber, army co-operation and reconnaissance. Despite the aeroplane's success, it did not receive a production order, any more than did the Type 120 which flew a year later on 29 January 1932. The Type 120 was bought by the Air Ministry however and used for research at Martlesham Heath while Type 118 returned to Filton as an engine flying test bed.

The Bristol Type 123 four-gun fighter (29ft 7in span, 695hp Rolls-Royce Goshawk III, 235 mph) was first flown on June 1934 by Captain Uwins. The engine was steam cooled and suffered numerous problems while lateral stability problems also persisited. On Uwins recommendation, the type was abandoned.

Interest in the single engine fighter now revived considerably. Air Ministry specification F7/30 called for a single-seat day and night fighter carrying four machine guns. The specification looked for higher performance and fire power than had ever been built into a British fighter but it went on to specifically call up the Rolls-Royce Goshawk engine, a development of the Kestrel which was cooled by an evaporative system. This latter installation was to prove the downfall of the Bristol designs in response to F7/30. The design itself, the Bristol Type 123 was an aggressive but heavy bi-plane, the last of that format to be produced at Bristol. With a cooling system buried in the leading edge of the wing and also partly in the fixed spatted undercarriage, the engine gave nothing but trouble from the day of its installation. Even on ground running, the system proved unsatisfactory and the aeroplane did not fly until 12 June 1934. When it did, Uwins expressed himself dissatisfied with just about every aspect of its performance and, even with the fin and rudder area substantially increased, lateral instability plagued the early flight tests. It was largely on Uwins' recommendation that Barnwell did not persist with the design and it was dropped. Fedden had already persuaded the Board to go for a radial engine answer to the specification as a private venture and this machine, a gull winged monoplane was following up quickly behind the bi-plane. It flew on 8 July 1934 and was found to be fast and manoeuvrable. Uwins pronounced himself content, even being heard to say that he thought the Company had a winner on its hands. The Type 133 is interesting historically as the first Bristol type to make full use of the recent development in the United States of America of aluminium alclad, an alloy of aluminium clad with pure aluminium on the surface, giving lightness and strength together with good anti-corrosive qualities. It was also the first fighter aircraft fitted with a retractable undercarriage and the first Bristol aircraft to exceed 300 m.p.h. Uwins and his team embarked on a test programme during which most of the handling trials were completed in only eighteen hours flying time. However they called for many improvements, including such changes as an enclosed cockpit and increased rudder area, so it was not until 8 March 1935 that the final spinning and

The Bristol Type 133 fighter (39ft span, 640hp Mercury VIS2, 260 mph) first flew to an Air Staff specification in June 1934 and proved extremely promising, until careless handling (not by Captain Uwins) caused a flat spin from 14,000ft from which the aircraft did not recover although the pilot escaped. No replacement was available.

The wreck of the Type 133 at Longwell Green on 8 March 1935.

diving tests took place. In the hands of a pilot named Campbell the Type 133 was put into a right hand spin at 14,000 feet over east Bristol and unfortunately the undercarriage had not been retracted. The aeroplane went into an uncontrollable flat spin from which Campbell was unable to recover. He baled out, just getting clear at 2000 feet while the aeroplane crashed at Longwell Green. As this was a private venture, only one prototype had been built and this ended Bristol's entry in the F7/30 contract.

In the meanwhile, great things had been happening in the engine world. Fedden had always been interested in high altitude performance and when in 1930, the Americans took the height record using a Wright Apache aeroplane and a Pratt and Whitney Wasp engine, he felt he could go one better. The American aeroplane was a special machine which mounted a second supercharger in the fuselage in addition to the one already fitted to the Wasp. Fedden's plan was to use a Pegasus S with no second supercharger. A Pegasus was taken from the production line at Patchway, fitted into a Vickers Vespa, a two-seat bi-plane and on 16 September 1932 was flown from Filton by Cyril Uwins to 43,976 feet. Uwins was provided with one of the first electrically heated flying suits and his face was covered in vaseline to protect him against the bitterly cold air at that altitude. The whole flight took two hours and started at 13.00 hours in brilliant sunshine with good visibility. The engine ran perfectly and the climb proceeded steadily but Uwins found considerable turbulence at the climax of the climb when the temperature was down at -57 degrees Celsius. The peak of the record attempt was reached after 103 minutes. Uwins was in an open cockpit, with no radio and only very primitive oxygen equipment.

Taking the world height record established Bristol as the one of two leading aircraft-engine manufacturers in Britain, the other being Rolls-Royce. Another project captured the public imagination in 1933, the Westland-Houston expedition to fly over the summit of Mount Everest, a considerable feat in those days. Fedden was approached by Lt Col L. D. Stewart Blacker, an aviation enthusiast, for advice on the best kind of engine to make the Everest flight. Fedden advised that the Pegasus would be completely suitable and the result was the successful flight over the summit on 3 April 1933. This was the first time that man had looked down on the highest point on this planet. Finance for the venture was supplied by Lady Houston, the philanthropist who had already financed the British Schneider Trophy team which won that prize outright in 1931. Blacker managed to get hold of two Westland aircraft, the PV machine and Wallace prototype and these aircraft, after testing in the United Kingdom, were shipped out to India. The two machines were put together with their Bristol engines, which performed faultlessly throughout the expedition. The Everest expedition was yet another spur to Bristol and Roy Fedden who pressed on remorselessly with the ever improving development of his engines. 1933 had seen the climb to power in Germany of Adolf Hitler and the appointment of Herman Goering as Minister of Aviation. Roy Fedden was among those who recognised that a European war could not be long delayed and all his efforts went in to producing the engines with which that war would be fought. Fedden made frequent trips to Germany and knew the German industrial scene intimately.

Captain Uwins' height record lasted for just one year until 28 September 1933 when a French aeroplane climbed 1000 ft higher, followed in the spring of 1934 by an Italian Caproni 161 going further still, using a Bristol Pegasus engine built under licence. This Italian achievement led to a British reaction. Captain Barnwell had already proposed to the Air Ministry a special high-altitude monoplane for research purposes. To this project he gave the Type number 138 and in June 1934, he was invited to tender for two aircraft to Specification 2/34. This resulted in the Type 138A which was fitted with a special Pegasus capable of flying above 50,000 ft and using a two-stage supercharger. Special pressure suits were commissioned from the Royal Aeronautical Establishment and the National Physical Laboratory.

The resulting aircraft and high altitude equipment were ready by the spring of 1936 and flight tested at Filton by Captain Uwins. The special Pegasus was not ready at this time so the machine was flight tested with a standard Pegasus, having the new engine fitted in August with its specially developed four-bladed propeller. A Royal Air Force pilot, Squadron Leader F.R.D. Swain was selected for the flight and on 28 September 1936 at 7.30 am he took off from Farnborough. He climbed to an officially certified height of 49,967 ft and returned to earth at the R.A.F. station at Netheravon in Wiltshire two hours after take off. The Italians replied by taking the record again at the beginning of 1937. The Bristol machine was overhauled and a few minor modifications incorporated to save weight, such as the removal of brakes and the fitting of smaller wheels. Another attempt was made on the record on 30 June 1937, the pilot being Flight Lieutenant M.J. Adam. This time the record was established at 53,937 ft and ended that round of Bristol's interest in the record. The Company would return to the attack in the 1950s.

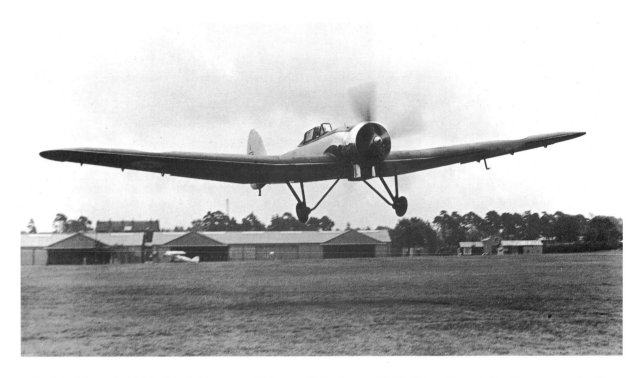

The Bristol Type 138A High Altitude Monoplane (66ft span, 500hp Pegasus PE 6X, 123 mph) was built with government backing for a British world height record attempt, one of Fedden's preoccupations in the early thirties. The machine twice broke the record on 28 September 1936 (49,967 ft) by Sqn Ldr F.R.D. Swain and again on 30 June 1937 (53,937 ft) by Fl Lt M.J. Adam.

Rolls-Royce

The four-bladed propeller and Pegasus engine installation for the Type 138 included a mechanical supercharger and separate booster which the pilot cut in at supreme height.

The following year, 1938, the Bristol Aeroplane Company added the world distance record to its other achievements. The R.A.F. had formed a Long Distance Flight using Barnes Wallis' Vickers Wellesley single-engined bomber, which employed Wallis' famous geodetic construction method. This aircraft used a Bristol Pegasus XXII engine which ran on 100 octane fuel and used one of the new Rotol 3-bladed propellers with variable pitch. On 5/6 November 1938, two Wellesleys left Ismailia in Egypt and flew non-stop 7162 miles in forty-eight hours five minutes to Darwin, Australia. The record stood for years and the Wellesley was one of 28 new types of aircraft in production that year using Bristol engines.

By the time the second height record attempt had been made in 1937, the transformation of the Bristol Aeroplane Company into the largest manufacturer of engines and airframes in Europe was well under way. Back in 1932 when the factory had been virtually empty of airframe orders, Barnwell's design office at that time was concerning itself with the Bristol Type 130, a bomber-transport to Air Ministry specification C26/31 which was scheduled to replace the antique Vickers Valentias which the R.A.F. were still operating in the Middle East and India. The resultant design was a twin-engined high wing monoplane using Pegasus Mark III engines. This machine was the largest to be built at Filton to date with a span of 96 ft. The aircraft was first flown on 23 June 1935 by Captain Uwins and following completion of its initial flight trials it was handed over to the R.A.F. at Martlesham where its test pilot was Flight Lieutenant A. J. Pegg, universally known as 'Bill'. This was Pegg's first direct contact with the Bristol Company. Later he would resign his commission to join Uwins' test pilot team at Filton and would eventually succeed him as Chief Test Pilot in 1947. The Type 130 succeeded in winning a production order and was officially named the Bristol Bombay in February 1937. By this time the Filton factory was so busy that there was no chance of such a large aeroplane going into quantity production, so a sub-contract for 50 machines was awarded to Short and Harland, a new company formed in Belfast by Short Brothers, who moved there from Rochester and the giant Harland and Wolff Shipbuilding Company who undertook to start up a Government-owned aircraft factory on Queen's Island.

By 1935, the Nazi Government in Germany had made its aggressive intentions plain, even to the British Government of Stanley Baldwin. This was the year that Britain determined to re-equip the Royal Air Force, unprecedented expansion took place in Bristol's aircraft factories in the years 1935-39. The sites at Filton and Patchway took the basic shape by which we know them today. The name of the Bristol Blenheim is one of the great names of British aviation and it was the development of this aircraft that caused the greatest expansion in the history of the Company. Yet it was not the British Government that took the first steps in the creation of the Blenheim but rather the ambitions of a newspaper tycoon and the never ending quest for technical perfection of the insatiable Fedden. To this must be added a long standing ambition of Frank Barnwell to produce a civil commercial light airliner capable of cruising speeds of at least 250 m.p.h.

Barnwell's idea for a twin-engined light airliner went back to 1933. He conceived a low-wing twin-engined monoplane with an enclosed cabin and accommodation for two pilots and six passengers. The aeroplane was to be equipped with two of the new sleeve valve engines that Fedden was developing at Patchway. Fedden's preoccupation with the sleeve valve went back to the early 1920s. Even at that time he had foreseen the day when the radial engine using poppet valves would be developed to a size and strength where the valve gear would become so complicated that further developments would be impractical. Ideas for sleeve valve engines had developed in the United States as early as the turn of the century. Two sleeves round the circumference of the cylinder rotated allowing fuel to enter through grilled vents, rather than the ever rattling valve stems, poppets, cams and valve gear of the conventional piston engine. The problem was that no one could mass produce sleeves to sufficient accuracy to guarantee a perfect circle.

Fedden's first engine was a nine-cylinder radial using cylinders of the same size as the Mercury. He named it the Perseus and it went ahead rapidly. It was the best looking engine that had been produced at Patchway and was an instant success. It had the advantage of being much quieter than the conventional engines and it proved to be more economic. In early 1933 Fedden instructed Frank Owner, who was by now in charge of future projects, to get down to a smaller sleeve valve engine for the airlines. This was the Aquila, capable of 450 h.p. and the engine which Frank Barnwell had specified for his Bristol Type 135 light airliner. Both the Perseus and Aquila turned out to be good engines but they had the disadvantage of being expensive to build because of the hand lapping of the sleeve valves. In October 1933 the Perseus IA became the first sleeve valve engine in the world to fly, going aloft in a Company Bulldog flown by Uwins as a flying test bed. Meanwhile Fedden pressed on with sleeve-valve development, his engineers

The Bristol Type 130 Bombay troop transport (95ft 9in span, 2 x 1010hp Pegasus XXII, 190 mph) was first flown on 23 June 1935, as a replacement for the RAF Vickers Valentias, and was the largest aircraft built at Filton to date. Due to lack of capacity at Filton works, 50 production models were built by Short and Harland at Belfast and were active in the Middle East theatre during the early years of the war, including the evacuation of the Greek royal family in 1941.

The classic series of sleeve-valve engines pioneered by Fedden in the thirties played a large part in British victory in the Second World War. The first into production was the 525hp Perseus, followed by the Aquila, Taurus, Hercules and Centaurus. The engine shown is preserved in Bristol.

and in particular Fred Whitehead, who had been with Fedden since Cosmos days, ever seeking the elusive production methods for mass quantities of sleeve valves.

Fate now took a hand. One evening in March 1934 Roy Fedden gave a lecture to the Bristol Motor Yacht Club at the Grand Spa Hotel in Clifton. When the meeting was over, Fedden was approached by Robert Lewis, editor of the *Bristol Evening World* newspaper. Lewis had been present at a lunch at which his boss, the English newspaper tycoon Lord Rothermere had mentioned seeing a mock-up of the Bristol Type 135 at the last Paris Air Show. Rothermere was anxious to commission 'the fastest commercial aeroplane in Europe' to rival

The famous Bristol Type 142 Britain First (56ft 4in span, 2650hp Mercury VIS2, 307 mph). Built as a private venture for the newspaper chief Lord Rothermere, it flew on 12 April 1935 and proved faster than any current fighter in service! It led to the Bristol series of twin-engined military aircraft, which served so well in the Second World War.

The sole example of the Bristol Type 143 light airliner (43ft 2in, 2 x 500hp Aquila I, 250 mph) which was powered by two of Fedden's early sleeve-valve engine, the Aquila, which was dropped in 1938.

the all-metal American machines which he had seen in the States. Bluntly, Fedden was asked by Lewis if the Bristol Company was capable of turning out such a machine. If so, Lewis said that Lord Rothermere would be interested. Fedden arranged to meet Lewis at Temple Meads station the following morning and travelled up to London to meet Rothermere. The two men got on immediately, Rothermere explaining his plans and Fedden returning the same day to Bristol to report to the Board.

Another version of this story claims that Lewis in the first instance approached Barnwell and that it was he who sketched out the initial version of the Rothermere aeroplane. Whichever version is correct, there is no doubt that Sir Stanley White, Barnwell and Fedden met Lord Rothermere in London on 29 March and that an agreement was reached that, for an estimated cost of £18,500, payable in two instalments, the Bristol Aeroplane Company would build Rothermere's required aeroplane. This was to have a crew of two and six passengers and fly at a speed quoted by Barnwell as 240 m.p.h. at 6500 ft. Barnwell pointed out that it would be necessary to fit Bristol Mercurys rather than Aquilas. It was an apprehensive Company Board that took on the Rothermere order, because it was fearful that the newspaper man had the real objective of embarrassing the Royal Air Force by producing a civil machine which was speedier than its fastest fighter. However, the Air Ministry reassured the Bristol Directors that they would be supportive of the new project and work on the machine went ahead. The Company also decided to build a twin Aquila-powered prototype side by side with the Rothermere aeroplane and the machines were given the Bristol type numbers 142 and 143.

Blenheims of the second production order for the R.A.F. under assembly in the Erecting Hall in late 1937.

When the type 142 made its first flight at Filton on 12 April 1935, it caused a sensation. It was 50 m.p.h. faster with full load than the R.A.F.'s new fighter, the Gloucester Gladiator. All who saw it and flew in it were highly impressed and Lord Rothermere presented it to the nation, having named it 'Britain First'. Barnwell in the meanwhile had schemed a bomber version of the machine and interest from the Air Ministry and from Finland was immediately expressed.

The Type 143 was delayed by having to wait for production versions of its Aquila engine and did not fly until 20 January 1936. It was retained by the Company as a test bed for the Aquila but this engine did not find a buyer and so the aircraft was laid up. Any intention to develop it as an airliner was prevented by the already large quantity of orders for the military version of 142 which the Company had received as early as August 1935.

By this time the British Government's plans for defence expansion had become public knowledge and the industry was preparing for a rapid expansion. To meet this challenge the Directors of the Bristol Aeroplane Company on 15 June 1935 'went public' with a share capital of £1,200,000. At the time there were 4200 people working for the Company, with the majority in the engine factory at Patchway. The Company received an order for 150 of the Blenheim Bomber, as the type 142M was named, in September 1935, and had received instructions from the Air Ministry to go ahead with further bi-planes, but not of their own design. Two batches of the Hawker Audax amounting to 141 aeroplanes were built and delivered during 1935 and early 1936. This allowed the Filton management to build up its manpower from the 4200 on the payroll in June to 8233 by Christmas. This labour force had to be trained in the manufacture of light alloy parts and many families moved from South Wales to Bristol. To support this expansion, the machine shop at Filton was enlarged as also was the tool room and the Erecting Hall, which had last been expanded in 1916, was doubled in size. A new Main Plane Department for the production of Blenheim wings went up alongside the Erecting Hall and new treatment and paint shops were also built.

At the same time, the architect Austin Hall, was commissioned to design a new headquarters for the Company. This was erected on a site alongside old Filton House just in front of the original tramway sheds and was ready for occupation by April 1936. This building, New Filton House, remained the site headquarters until 1996. An attractive building with a statue of Pegasus on its northern side, it contains much glass work in the art deco style so characteristic of the 1930s.

A wide internal road was built from the Erecting Hall down Filton Hill to the airfield and as the years progressed towards 1939, other buildings sprang up down the hill including two sub-assembly shops and a large experimental department. At the foot of the hill three flight sheds came into existence. The demand for aero engines also trebled at this time. With considerable foresight, the Bristol Board had bought up land on the eastern side of the A38 highway and now this was put into use. Until 1935 the only building on the eastern side of the road had been the engine factory canteen but now a new production plant of 200,000 sq. ft. was complete by 1936. Additional test facilities sprang up and on the south side of the airfield a specialist factory to deal in aircraft cowlings and exhaust systems came into being and was named after a nearby house, Rodney Works. When war broke out in September 1939 the Bristol Aeroplane Company possessed the largest single aircraft factory in the world, covering a total area of land of 732 acres, compared with just 13 acres a few years earlier.

All this expansion at Filton and Patchway drew new employees into the area and was the direct cause of new building in the surrounding communities. The City of Bristol had spread out earlier in the century along the Gloucester Road forming the communities of Bishopston and Horfield. Now Filton itself underwent a metamorphosis as new houses sprang up along Filton Avenue and the new roads that led off. Filton became one of the typical new suburbs of the '30s – semi-detached houses with pleasant gardens, all reflecting the new-found prosperity that the aircraft business had brought to the neighbourhood. Further north at Patchway overspill housing development from Bristol took shape in the form of Patchway Estate. Here again the emphasis was on spaciousness and semi-detached houses, a far cry from the rows of terraces that the new residents had known in the east of Bristol or in the valleys of South Wales.

Despite the expansion in 1935, if aircraft production was to achieve anything like numerical equality with Germany, further manufacturing facilities would have to be developed. There was no possibility of expanding the existing aircraft factories at an even greater rate. They had achieved miracles enough. So the proposal to build 'shadow factories' emerged in the early part of 1936 with the selection of the Bristol

*The new Bristol Aeroplane Company headquarters, New Filton House which was completed by April 1936
to the designs of architect Austin Hall. It contains much art deco work of the period.*

Mercury as the first engine to be produced outside the aircraft industry. The British motor car industry, which was well established by this time, was the obvious candidate. A shadow factory was built at Patchway alongside the East Works and used as a pattern for other factories, mainly built in the Midlands. Fedden had already established an apprentice training school and college at Patchway in 1934 and many of the emerging young engineers later found work in the shadow factories, usually at junior and middle management level. The proposal for the shadow factories originated with the Air Staff and particularly with the late Air Chief-Marshal Sir Hugh Dowding, who would go on to command Fighter Command in the Battle of Britain. In Fedden, Dowding found an immediate response and the great designer turned his attention to convincing the motor car industry that they could in fact produce the Mercury. Daimler, the Rootes Group, Rover, Standard and Austin all took part in the shadow factory scheme for engines and others would join later. At the outbreak of war 51,000 people were working in shadow factories producing engines, which by this time included large numbers of the Pegasus and the first batches of the new sleeve-valve Hercules.

The shadow factories scheme was extended in 1937 to include aircraft and orders were placed for Blenheims with the Rootes-Hillman factory at Speke outside Liverpool. A contract for Blenheims also went to A.V. Roe at Chadderton near Manchester – a factory which today co-operates very closely with Filton on Airbus wing production. Later in the war, shadow factories would be set up at Oldmixon near Weston-super-Mare and at Accrington in Lancashire.

Another project that came from the fertile mind of Fedden in these hectic years was the establishment of a reliable supply of aircraft propellers. Fedden had made propellers at Patchway in the early '30s but never obtained the quality that he sought. In 1937 he persuaded the Bristol Board to set up a new propeller company in co-operation with Rolls-Royce. Fedden found a ready response to his scheme from E. W. Hives of Rolls and the joint factory was established at Staverton on the main A40 road between

*Bristol Blenheim IV, Type 149 (56ft 4in span, 2 x 920hp Mercury, 295 mph) of
No. 18 Squadron R.A.F. in 1941. 7212 Blenheims and derivatives were built.*

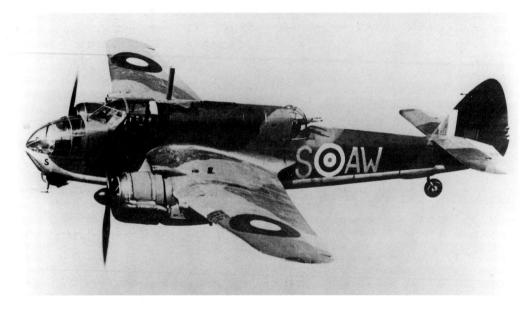

*The Bristol Type 152 Beaufort torpedo bomber (57ft 10in span, 2 x 1130hp Taurus VI, 260 mph) first flew on
15 October 1938, having already been ordered into production. 1429 aircraft were built in Filton or Banwell,
while Australia built 700 using Pratt and Whitney Twin Wasps.*

*The Bristol Type 146 eight-gun fighter (39ft, 840hp Mercury IX, 287 mph) was built to AM Spec. F5/34 and
flew in 1938 but was already outdated by the Hurricane and Spitfire, with their Merlin engines.*

The Army Co-operation monoplane Type 148 (40ft span, 840hp Mercury IX, 255 mph) which flew in October 1937 but lost out to the Westland Lysander for production orders.

Gloucester and Cheltenham. The new company was called Rotol and was producing airscrews by the end of 1937. It would go on to produce nearly all the propellers that sustained the Royal Air Force in the Second World War and become a famous name in world aviation. Its basic product was an hydraulic piston-driven feathering propeller. A much developed form of this airscrew remains in production today in the company that is now owned by BLC Dowty.

The Patchway factory was supplying engines for a variety of new aircraft. Among the most famous in the civil aviation world was the Short Empire flying boat, which first took to the air from the Medway on 3 July 1936, using four Bristol Pegasus Xc. This S23 flying boat was a joint venture between Imperial Airways and the British Government to place a modern airmail machine on the routes to India and Australia. It was an all-metal, twin-decked, attractive looking aircraft and in February 1937 one of the class, the 'Caledonia', initiated air routes between Ireland and Newfoundland, setting up the first transatlantic air routes. The Empire flying boat was another sign of the emergence of Great Britain from the depression years and was viewed by the general public as an equally important national status symbol as the liner *Queen Mary*. It appeared on all kinds of publicity in the late '30s and its Bristol engines enjoyed a considerable reputation.

The first prototype Bristol Blenheim bomber, the Type 142M, took off from Filton on its first flight with Captain Uwins at the controls on 25 June 1936. By this time production was in full swing and enquiries had been received from Finland, Turkey and Yugoslavia. The Air Ministry agreed to the sale of the machine to friendly countries once the requirements of the R.A.F. were met. Supplies to the squadrons began in March 1937, the first copies going to No. 114 Squadron at R.A.F. Wyton. By 1938 over 700 Blenheims were on order and in April the Government of Finland acquired a licence to produce the aircraft in that country. The original 18 Blenheims supplied to Finland fought valiantly against the Red Air Force in the Winter War of 1940 and the type was also manufactured in Yugoslavia, the rate of Blenheim production accelerated to such a pitch that by December 1937 Filton was turning out 24 aircraft every month.

Hardly was Blenheim production under way in September 1935 when the Air Staff issued a specification for a twin-engined torpedo bomber. The Bristol design office began to scheme a submission for the contract which used a considerable number of Blenheim components, based on the same design philosophy. A slightly larger aircraft all round, the Beaufort was planned to use the Perseus engine but it was found necessary to fit the larger, more powerful Taurus. This specification had been issued in parallel with one for a similar aircraft which required the torpedo to be carried completely inside the machine. The Bristol team managed to convince the Air Ministry that this was unnecessary but the Air Staff still insisted on a crew of four and so the Beaufort appeared as a fairly chunky aeroplane. Later on the Company would prove that torpedo bombing could be quite easily carried out by a crew of two when the Beaufighter torpedo bomber was developed during the Second World War. The Beaufort was flight tested by Uwins at Filton on 15 October 1938. It was the third prototype to fly from the air field that year, the others being the Type 146 fighter and the Type 148 Army Co-operation machine. The 146 was a handy little fighter powered by a Mercury IX but soon outclassed by the Spitfire and Hurricane. It performed perfectly but was damaged in an accident at Filton Air Display in 1938 and was scrapped as beyond repair. The type 148 was produced to the same specification as the famous Westland Lysander and did not get a production order.

This summer of 1938 which was to climax in the Munich crisis saw the Bristol Aeroplane Company suffer a tragic loss. While Captain Barnwell was recognised as one of the great aircraft designers the same could not be said for his skills as a pilot. He had experienced a number of crashes in his time but always managed to escape relatively uninjured. By the 1930s he was considered by the Company to be uninsurable and it became necessary to 'ground' him. He accepted the decision apparently without complaint although it did not stop him taking over the controls of aeroplanes other than those that belonged to the Company. So it was that in 1938 he proposed a scheme for a light aircraft to equip the Civil Air Guard, a scheme to train amateur pilots as potential recruits available for aircrew if war broke out. Barnwell devised a light aeroplane which he called his BSWI. The B stood for Barnwell, the S for the Scott 25 h.p. motor cycle engine that powered the little monoplane and W stood simply for Whitchurch. The aircraft was of all-wood construction and built by a syndicate of aircraft employees in one of the sheds at the Bristol City Airport at Whitchurch. The aeroplane flew for the first time in Barnwell's hands on 30 July. Barnwell decided that the machine was not quite right, made some adjustments and took it into the air in the evening of 2 August. Just after Barnwell had made his first turn the machine stalled and spun straight in from about 100 ft. This time there was no walking away uninjured and one of this country's greatest aviation experts lay dead in the wreckage. His memory is recalled today by the annual Barnwell Memorial Lectures arranged by the Royal Aeronautical Society and by the evergreen reputation of his aircraft – the Fighter, the Bulldog and the Blenheim.

Barnwell was succeeded as Chief Designer by Leslie Frise, who in his turn was succeeded as Technical Designer by a rising star at Filton, the thirty-four year old Archibald Russell. Russell was born in May 1904 and after being educated at Fairfield School and Bristol University, joined Barnwell's design organisation in 1926. By 1931 he had risen to be Chief Technician and now took over the development of the

Leslie G. Frise who joined the company in 1916 and succeeded Barnwell as Chief Engineer in 1938. He was greatly involved in the Bulldog, Blenheim and Brabazon. Frise left Bristol for Percival in 1946 and then went to Blackburn Aircraft in 1956. He died in Bristol in September 1979.

The Filton Stress Office in 1937, A.E.Russell in the centre of the front row with Fred Pollicut on his left.

The rugged Type 156 Beaufighter (57ft 10in span, 2 x 1400hp Hercules, 330 mph) twin-engined fighter which served in a variety of roles throughout the Second World War and was known as the 'Whispering Death' to Japanese ground troops.

The thousandth aircraft, a Beaufighter, to come from the Weston factories. At peak production, these plants were producing 90 Beaus a month. 5564 Beaufighters were built in England and a further 364 in Australia.

Blenheim, Beaufort and the new fighter which Frise was currently scheming. The famous Beaufighter has been called an 'inspired stop-gap'. The Type 156 Beaufighter owed its conception to the failure over a period of 1937 and '38 of the industry to produce a powerful canon armed fighter for escort and ground attack duties. Because four cannon firing at once cause aero-dynamic problems when placed in juxtaposition to the power generated by two Hercules engines, it took a considerable time to devise an acceptable layout. The spin-off from these arguments resulted in the unsatisfactory Armstrong Whitworth Albemarle bomber and the turret fighter, the Boulton Paul Defiant. Both these aircraft were produced in limited quantities but did not prove satisfactory in service. The Beaufighter used twin-Hercules engines and four cannon and was built around the wings, undercarriage and tail surfaces of the Beaufort, the two sets of equipment being virtually interchangeable. Such was the sense of urgency and the speed of the work at Filton in getting this much needed aircraft into the air – it was the time of the Munich crisis – that only six months elapsed between the first layout schemes and the first flight of the aeroplane on 17 July 1939.

Many of the delays to good aircraft in the British aircraft industry have occurred because design organisations could not get drawings out to programme. The story of the Beaufighter is a brilliant example of a drawing office using existing components and economical methods to get a prototype into the air. In the event only 2100 drawings were needed to produce the prototype Beaufighter. When allied to the new Hercules sleeve-valve engine, the new aircraft was designed to be as fast at 335 m.p.h. as any of the Hawker Hurricane fighters then flying.

By the time the Beaufighter got into the air the Bristol Hercules sleeve-valve radial engine was in full production at Patchway, its 1938 power rating being 1375 h.p. The development of the sleeve-valve engine had been a close run thing but it was Fedden's greatest technical achievement. Between July 1932 and the same month of 1938 Fedden ran five sleeve-valve designs, all increasing in power. His first complete sleeve-valve engine was the Perseus which first ran in July 1932. It proved a successful engine and was

Rolls-Royce

*The mighty Centaurus which first ran at Patchway in 1938 and became Britain's
most powerful radial engine, eventually developing up to 2625 hp per unit. It more than
held its own with early jet engines and, in the Korean War, a Centaurus-powered
Hawker Sea Fury is credited with shooting down a jet powered Mig 15!*

delivered in quantity, being used by Imperial Airways on civilian services by June 1935 and employed to re-engine the R.A.F.'s rather ancient Vickers Vildebeeste IV torpedo bombers in 1937. Its successor, the nine-cylinder Aquila was used in the Bristol light airliner, the Type 142, in 1934 but it did not go into production. The next Fedden sleeve-valve was the Hercules which was run in January 1936. A much larger engine, it used 14 cylinders of the same type as used in the Perseus and the prototype produced over 1000 h.p. It emerged as a slim looking engine with many improvements including much better fuel quality. The Hercules would be made in quantity, production being nearly 60,000 engines and, after the Second World War, would be built in France in large quantities by SNECMA.

The Pegasus was followed up very quickly in November 1936 by the first prototype of the Taurus. The aim of this design was to obtain a compact engine, at only 47 inches in diameter, producing 1065 h.p. It was the engine that was selected to give more power for the Beaufort and went into production for this aircraft. It was also used to power the Fairey Albacore, the planned successor to the venerable Swordfish. In the event the Swordfish, powered by a Mercury, turned out to be the better aeroplane.

What was to prove Fedden's final and greatest engine produced in quantity was the Bristol Centaurus. Everything about the Centaurus was big. It had 18 cylinders and was first run in July 1938. By 1939 this wonderful engine was already producing 2000 h.p. but did not get into action until the middle of the war in the Hawker Tornado fighter. Then it came into its own as probably the best aircraft engine of its type in the world.

So it was that Fedden and the team at Bristol backed by a far-seeing and courageous Board, had supplied the Royal Air Force with conventional and sleeve-valve engines such as the Mercury, the Hercules, the Taurus and the Centaurus that were the equal of anything produced elsewhere. The low maintenance required, the tough operating qualities and the power delivered by the Bristol sleeve-valve engines was never exceeded by any other motor, particularly by anything that came from Germany. This was just as well for one month and seventeen days after the first flight of the Bristol Beaufighter, the Royal Air Force found itself at war with dedicated pilots of Goering's Luftwaffe. Fedden's engines had arrived not a moment too soon.

5

THE WINGS OF WAR

1939 – 1945

*'This cursed ... war from the air has revolutionised our position.
We are not the same kind of country we used to be when
we were an island, only twenty years ago.'*

Winston S. Churchill, House of Commons, February 1934.

On 3 September 1939, the British ultimatum to the German Government remained unanswered. The deadline was 11.00 a.m. on an autumn Sunday morning and only one hour and three minutes passed before a Bristol Blenheim IV of 139 Squadron took off from the R.A.F. station at Wyton with orders to find the ships of the German fleet off the naval port of Wilhemshaven at the entrance to the Kiel Canal. The Blenheim reached its objective despite haze and mist but a radio failure prevented any details of the naval force being transmitted back to a waiting force of other Blenheims which were preparing to attack the warships. This single Blenheim arrived safely back at base at ten minutes to five, having carried out the first operational flight of the Second World War by the R.A.F.

By the outbreak of war, the R.A.F. had 1089 Blenheims on charge. Of these 240 were in the Middle East or Far East and over 300 Maintenance Units in store. There were probably 350 Blenheims available for immediate service in the Squadrons and Bristol engines were power units for Bomber Command's front line force of 169 Handley Page Hampdens and 160 Vickers Wellingtons.

The people of Bristol received early warning of the approaching war when, in August 1939, a decision was taken to disperse the fleets of British Airways and Imperial Airways from their headquarters outside London at Croydon and Hendon and bring them to Whitchurch, Bristol's civic airport. The big machines of the two national airlines were sitting targets for German bombers and Whitchurch was considered to be a safer centre of operations for the airline's De Havilland Albatross and the giant HP42 bi-planes. The British Overseas Airways Corporation (BOAC) had been formed from British Airways and Imperial Airways in June 1939, just two months before the outbreak of war. Whitchurch now entered the busiest period of its history. Before 1939 trade had taken some time to build up. In 1936 a significant event was the arrival of the first air service from Ireland. In addition to the Irish, Rail Air Services, Channel Air Ferries, Great Western Airlines and Southern Airlines all joined Western Airways to run services out of Whitchurch. Well before the outbreak of war, Bristol had an airlink with most major British cities.

Towards the end of 1938 a R.A.F. training unit arrived at Whitchurch with 12 machines and additional hangars were built to cater for the aircrews and associated staff and equipment. The aircraft were Hawker Harts and Tiger Moths. By the spring of 1939 these had risen in number to 26. The City Council carried out many improvements to the airport in the immediate pre-war period.

Whitchurch would see many exciting events during the war. None was more dramatic than when, in the bitter winter of early 1940, two of the giant Handley Page 42 bi-planes *Heracles* and *Hanno* were demolished in a gale and had to be written off. Then, a Luftwaffe raid on 20 December 1940, destroyed the De Havilland Albatross prototype *Frobisher*, arguably the most beautiful of all airliners before or since.

After the invasion of the Netherlands in May 1940, Royal Dutch Airlines (K.L.M.) based their D.C.3 unit at Whitchurch, and maintained the U.K.-Lisbon shuttle, so important to wartime diplomacy. This service was tacitly ignored by the Germans until October 1943 when a homeward-bound K.L.M. D.C.3 was

The Bristol aircraft factories in a Luftwaffe photograph of 1940.

A group of women trimmers in the Dope Shop in the Second World War.

shot down in the Bay of Biscay by Ju.88s in the mistaken impression that Churchill was on board. In fact, the aircraft was carrying film star Leslie Howard, returning from promoting his film *First of the Few* in Portugal.

In the City itself, the organisation of A.R.P. civil defence was placed in the hands of the City's Emergency Committee under the leadership of Alderman Frank Parrish as Chairman with Alderman Sir John Inskip as his Conservative Vice Chairman. At Filton, a camouflage scheme covered the whole factory. All the buildings were covered with a kaleidoscope of turgid brown, green and black paint which was supposed to give the impression of an open landscape to any passing aircraft. In poor weather conditions, this camouflage paint may well have helped to hide the aircraft plants but in sunshine, particularly in early morning or evening, the factory on the side of the hill at Filton made a tempting target for any passing Luftwaffe squadron.

Arrangements had to be made for the daily transport to Filton at the height of the war of 37,000 people working at the aircraft factory and also at Patchway. Shift working was introduced and the Bristol Tramway Company performed miracles with relays of buses twenty-four hours, seven days a week. The workers' return fare from the Centre to Filton, a distance of five miles each way, cost three old pennies. At the height of the war, the flat rate for a skilled fitter for a forty-eight hour week was 66s 6d. This could be improved by one third under the factory's incentive bonus scheme. A great deal of overtime was also available. A Filton veteran, Harold Lewis, recalls that when he joined the Company at the age of fifteen and a half in 1939 his weekly pay was 13s 3d, advancing by stages to 18s 5d at the age of eighteen.

The Royal Air Force possessed more Blenheims than any other type at the outbreak of war, although the Beaufort had by now replaced it on the assembly lines at Filton. Nevertheless, constant action produced many damaged aircraft which required repair and by April 1940, the Aircraft Service Department had been expanded to meet the demand of the service for repaired aircraft. Minor repairs were carried out by Bristol working parties travelling to R.A.F. stations as needed. R.A.F. personnel were also brought to Filton in large numbers for training at the Company's service school, the airframe school at Avonmouth and the engine school located in the Bristol Blind School at Henleaze. Sub-contractors were found to repair aircraft at strategic points nationwide, there being contractors in Surrey, Glamorgan, Lancashire and the Clyde Valley at Renfrew. Badly damaged aeroplanes were dismantled and brought back to Filton for repair in the jigs there. 6578 Bristol-designed aerolanes were repaired and returned to service satisfactorily between 1939 and 1945 and of these, 1200 were repaired on service airfields by Filton working parties.

The Flying School was transferred to Staverton between Gloucester and Cheltenham on 3 August 1940. By this time enemy action over the United Kingdom was intense and a balloon barrage was established over north Bristol. While these great monsters gave comforting psychological uplift to the local population, they never really proved a hazard to raiding Luftwaffe. A second flying school had been operated under Bristol management at Yatesbury in Wiltshire from January 1936 moving to Weston-super-Mare in September 1940. The Bristol Flying School also operated at Yatesbury from October 1939, flying De Havilland Dominies. The Company maintained this school throughout the war, training 18,500 wireless operators for the R.A.F. All closed at the end of the war but the Company negotiated a new reserve school contract in 1948 and continued training for the R.A.F. until March 1953.

The second reason for dispersal from Filton was the number of employees working on aircraft production as the war progressed. In 1942 there were 52,095 personnel on the payroll, including the shadow factories at Banwell and Accrington. But it was the Luftwaffe that caused the greatest evacuation from the Filton site.

The war opened quietly in Bristol. By the early months of 1940, people began to regard the air-raid sirens as something of a joke and many carried on with their normal duties when the familiar wail went off. Bristol did not get its first night visit from the Luftwaffe until 24 June 1940. By this time the factory was surrounded by the balloon barrage and there were anti-aircraft guns at strategic points. A set of heavy guns on the Purdown Ridge could fire at all angles across the City. Five people were killed in central Bristol in the raid of the night of 24/25 June 1940 but the factory was not touched. The training of a civil defence contingent of volunteers from the workforce continued during the summer and the Company's fire and ambulance services were also expanded. On 4 July a lone He. III bomber penetrated the defences in daytime and two bombs fell. Again there was no damage to the factory. Neither was there on 14 August when three Ju. 88 fighter bombers came in just as the day shift was ending. The local anti-aircraft guns drove them off and two were intercepted by Hurricane fighters from Chivenor. The Filton and Patchway factories were clearly a prime target for the 3rd Air Fleet of General Albert Kesselring based in Northern France. The Battle of Britain was at its height and very few days passed in this summer of 1940 without work being interrupted with air raid warnings. The Company introduced its own air raid warning system using the local Royal Observer Corps posts to give the alarm when it appeared the factory was about to be attacked. Following night raids on 17 and 22 August 1940, when superficial damage was caused to both factories, the major blow to Filton took place on 25 September 1940.

Girls rivetting up an outer wing spar for a Bristol Beaufighter in the Second World War.

Girls fitting out a Bristol Beaufort with engine installation during the Second World War.

Girls manning electric trucks to supply departments for factory communications during the Second World War.

A strong force of Heinkels swept in over Avonmouth and bombed the factory from south-west to north-east. In all 72 employees were killed outright and a further 19 died from their wounds. Another 147 were injured. The factory was out of action for ten days but then the Beaufighter production lines started rolling again and remained uninterrupted for the rest of the war. For a raid which succeeded in its objective, the damage was far less than expected. Three of the raiding Heinkels were shot down by the local anti-aircraft guns and more were most likely intercepted by Fighter Command before they could return to France.

A memorial to the dead of this raid, placed at the entrance to the site headquarters in Filton House, is now in Filton church.

The effects of this raid were immediate. The following day No. 118 Squadron arrived at Filton with its Hawker Hurricane fighters and when Kesselring tried a second attack on 27 September, the Hurricanes scrambled and drove the raiders away. There were no hits on the factory. The outcome was the immediate dispersal of all design staffs and non-essential personnel from the Filton production site. Filton House staff from Head Office moved to Clifton, together with parts of the design office which also had another establishment at Clevedon. Other places used were in Somerset at Highbridge, Wells and Whitchurch and such diverse buildings as a cider mill, a chocolate factory of Messrs Frys at Somerton and a bus garage were used for production shops. By the autumn of 1940, the Beaufighter Shadow Factory at Oldmixon, near Weston-super-Mare was ready for production. When Beaufighter orders ended in 1944 the factory went on to build the Hawker Tempest fighter, powered by Fedden's radials. The 25 September 1940 raid was the last attack on Filton which caused any damage although the City of Bristol was to suffer much in the next twelve months, the real blow falling on 24 November 1940. In six hours of destruction, much of the heart of old Bristol was torn out.

Aircraft shelters for production staff being dug at Filton immediately prior to the outbreak of war in 1939.
On 25 September 1940, two of these took direct hits from German bombs and 91 deaths resulted.

The City Docks area was damaged and Charles Hill's Shipyard hit. Two hundred people died. Other raids took place on 2 December and 6th. In all, Bristol suffered 76 aerial attacks during the 1939-45 war and 1299 citizens died. Another 2,602 were injured. Despite this, morale remained high and productivity soared. When the Home Guard was formed in 1940, two battalions, the 13th and 18th City of Bristol Home Guard, Gloucestershire Regiment were recruited entirely from employees of the Bristol Aeroplane Company. Another Bristol Aeroplane contribution to the war effort was the continual supply of blood donors provided by employees. In response to an emergency call from the Second Army just after D-Day in June 1944, the blood of 664 Bristol employees was flown direct from Filton to Normandy. In the first week of the invasion, a total of 2498 employees had given blood, 95% of the total supply sent across the Channel in that week.

The three major Bristol aircraft to serve the R.A.F. during the Second World War were the Blenheim, the Beaufort and the Beaufighter. The Blenheim had been largely phased out by 1944. By then two variants had been produced in quantities. In 1938 Bristol placed a contract with the Fairchild Aircraft Company based in Montreal, Canada for 97 copies of a Blenheim development which was given the Type No. 149 and named Bolingbroke. It was to all intents and purposes a Blenheim Mark IV and it could be operated on floats or skis if necessary. At the outbreak of war the project was taken over by the Canadian

Government and in all 676 machines were built. In service the Bolingbroke was used by the Royal Canadian Air Force for coastal patrol on its Atlantic and Pacific seaboards. It was also used for training and many bomber pilots got their first experience of multi-engined flying in Bolingbrokes in the Canadian training schools. Another Blenheim variant was flight tested by Captain Uwins at Filton for the first time on 24 February 1941. This was an up-rated Blenheim, originally called the Bisley and given the Type No. 160. The name was dropped in favour of Blenheim V and the machine carried greatly improved armament. It went into action during the Allied invasion of North Africa in November 1942 and later served in the Far East.

The Beaufort served from 1940 when it was prominent in the Norwegian campaign because of its long range. The Beaufighter, as the war progressed, became one of the most formidable fighting aeroplanes on any side. As we have seen, the Beaufighter was developed quickly in 1939 to give the R.A.F. a heavily armed fighter. It proved superb in a number of rôles and was rapidly converted into a night-fighting version during the German bomber offensive in the winter of 1940/41. Armed with a nose battery of 420mm cannon and 6.303 Browning machine guns in the wings, the Beaufighter was fitted with an early form of radar which gave it early and rapid success against German night raiders. It also appeared as a long range escort and fighter bomber in which it was particularly effective in strikes against German coastal shipping. In its final version it appeared as a torpedo bomber, carrying an 18-inch torpedo. It was in Burma, during tactical support operations of the British 14th Army that the Beaufighter earned the name of 'Whispering Death' from the Japanese.

Four Victoria Crosses were earned in Bristol aircraft during the Second World War and all of them between April 1941 and December 1942. The first was awarded posthumously to Flying Officer Kenneth Campbell of No. 22 Squadron, operating from St Eval in Cornwall, flying a Beaufort, Serial No. N1016, who torpedoed the German battleship *Gneisenau* in Brest on 6 April 1941.

On 4 July 1941 Squadron Leader Hugh Idwall Edwards, flying a Blenheim IV Serial No. V6028 of 105 Squadron from R.A.F. Swanton Morley, led a daylight raid by Blenheims on the German port of Bremen. The ground defences were more than usually active and Edwards received the V. C. for the leadership he showed in this and previous attacks and for the success of the raid. The next Victoria Cross was won on the second day of the Far Eastern War on 9 December 1941 during the early stages of the Japanese invasion of Malaya by Flight Lieutenant Arthur Stewart King Scarf of 62 Squadron operating in a Blenheim Mark I Serial No. L1134, flying a lone attack from the airfield at Butterworth in Northern Malaya. The final Victoria Cross earned in a Bristol aeroplane was posthumously won on 4 December 1942 by Squadron Leader Hugh Gordon Malcolm, the commanding officer of No. 18 Squadron. He led his Squadron in a Blenheim V Serial No. BA875 from a desert air strip at Souk-el-Arba near Blida in Algeria.

Success in developing twin-engined military aircraft was carried on by the Filton design team as the war progressed. Two further aeroplanes designed for the military rôle were produced, although there was no new prototype for Captain Uwins to fly from February 1941, when he flew the Bisley, to 4 February 1943 when he took off in the first prototype Bristol Buckingham, a four-seat high speed day bomber given the Bristol Type No. 163 and powered by two of the powerful new Centaurus engines. By the time the Buckingham had flown, the daylight role for air bombing had passed decisively to the American B17s of the U.S. 8th Air Force, and the Buckingham was never employed as a bomber. Rather it was developed as the Type 166 Buckmaster, for training or as a fast transport. The idea of a fast military transport developed into a famous design, the Bristol Type 170 Freighter/Wayfarer which was under development at Filton as the war ended. Concurrently with the Type 170 the final Second World War military design the Bristol Type 164 Brigand was also in production. This was a tough, fast (360 m.p.h.), long range (2800 miles with drop tanks) replacement for the Beaufighter but only two had been delivered when the war ended. The Brigand was planned for use in the Far East and when it eventually saw operational service with the R.A.F. in Malaya in the early '50s, it proved to be a tough and useful aeroplane. The remaining major wartime product in the Aircraft Division at Filton was the design to specification B.l/39 for a long-range four-engine bomber capable of striking at Berlin with a bomb load of 10,000lbs and a speed of 300 m.p.h. This design study became the Bristol Type 159. It never proceeded beyond the early design stage, but the early studies eventually developed into the monster Brabazon airliner.

We must now return to the Patchway factory and the wartime activities of Roy Fedden and his design team. At Patchway, the war began with 16,600 employees on the payroll. Roy Fedden and his original 30 men had grown into a large organisation which by this time had delivered 26,000 aeroplane engines which had been sold worldwide. The production of Pegasus, Mercury, Taurus and Hercules engines was

*The Bristol Buckingham B.I. light bomber (71ft 10in span, 2 x 2400hp Centaurus IV,
335 mph) arrived too late to be used effectively and was converted to a four-seat
high speed transport. Only 123 were built and most scrapped soon afterwards.*

*The Bristol Type 166 Buckmaster T.I. (71ft 10in span, 2 x 2400hp Centaurus,
352 mph) was a version of the Buckingham developed and used for
training by the R.A.F. in the late '40s. 112 were built.*

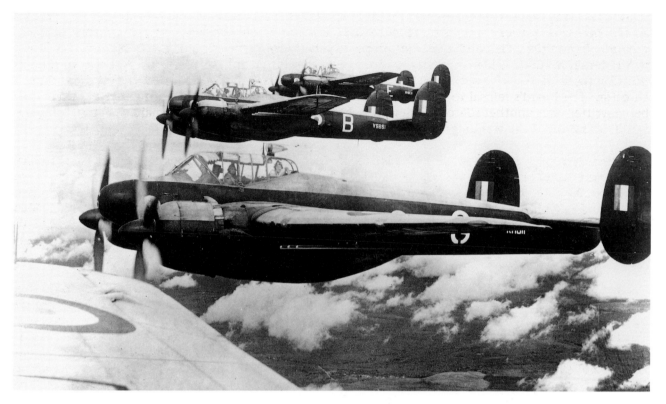

The rugged Bristol Type 164 Brigand (72ft 4in span, 2 x 2500hp Centaurus 57, 360 mph)
proved itself as a ground attack bomber in the difficult climatic conditions during the
Malayan emergency. The type went into service in 1949 and 147 were built at Filton.

in full swing. More importantly, development of the big 18-cylinder Centaurus was going ahead and Bristol was at its peak as a dominating factor in the world aero-engine market.

Development of the Centaurus, which was type tested in October 1939 for a delivery of 2000 h.p. was delayed by Ministry of Supply preference for the in-line engine. Much of the delay arose from the personal differences between Fedden and the Controller at the Minister of Supply, Air Chief Marshal Sir Wilfred Freeman. Freeman is alleged to have far preferred Rolls-Royce in-line engines to the Bristol radials and consequently failed to lend his support to the development of the Centaurus. This three-cornered fencing between Rolls, Bristol and the Ministry went on from 1940 to 1943. The failure of the Rolls-Royce Vulture engine led to the inevitable fitting of a Centaurus in the Hawker Tornado which flew in June 1940 as the Tempest. This combination of Sidney Camm's airframe and Fedden's engine proved to be one of the best fighters of the war. Developed as the Hawker Sea Fury, it flew with the Fleet Air Arm in the Korean War of 1950-52 and, in favourable circumstances, was able to take on the early version of the Russian Mig 15 jet fighter.

By the time the Tempest was airborne, a radical and dramatic change had taken place in the Patchway hierarchy.

Roy Fedden had begun the war with his customary energy, attempting to set up a Centaurus manu-facturing plant in the United States, spending hours closeted with Lord Beaverbrook, the new Minister of Aircraft Production and turning down a direct order from Churchill to take over the responsibility for the whole of British aero-engine manufacture. This remarkable man continued to work a twenty-hour day, devoting his attention entirely to a myriad of small parts such as circlips on the one hand and essential features like propeller shafts on the other, expecting his staff to work at the same pace and forcing many into early graves.

This period saw Fedden growing further apart from the Bristol Board. Sir William Verdon-Smith had already brought in Norman Rowbotham to run the production side at Patchway. He was now worried by Fedden's refusal to exercise prudent financial control over the many projects and there was also an acrimonious dispute about the size of royalties Fedden drew on every engine that the Company sold. Fedden's royalty contract went back to the Jupiter of 1922 which sold for £1000. Now the engines were selling for many times that figure and Fedden's royalty cheque had ascended astronomically. Fedden agreed that the contract should be re-negotiated but the whole incident left an unfortunate background. In addition, Fedden had earlier proposed a basic re-organisation of the Company and sent it to Sir Stanley White. Fedden correctly held the view that his engine department was the main prop of the Company in the 1930s and certainly resented the failure of the Board ever to appoint him a Director. The Board's refusal to implement Fedden's proposals, and their resentment at the letter ever being written, was another source of grievance. Nevertheless, he did agree to remain with the Company for the duration of the war and for six months after the end of hostilities.

These differences continued while the Luftwaffe campaign against Bristol in 1940 was at its height. The 25 September raid struck the engine department just as badly as the aircraft division at Filton. One 500 lb bomb scored a direct hit on a shelter at Rodney and 25 engine department employees were killed. In the midst of all this disruption, Fedden's active mind was scheming yet another new engine. This was to be his Orion, another large radial delivering 4000 h.p; a logical development to his range of piston engines and the kind of engine needed to power large bombers if the war went on for any length of time.

The decision to proceed with the Orion throws into perspective Fedden's approach to the gas turbine. As early as 1931, the young Frank Whittle, British pioneer of the gas turbine, had met Fedden and set out his proposals. Frank Owner, senior designer on Fedden's staff, had very strongly supported Whittle's ideas. Yet Fedden, so progressive in most things to do with aero-engines, viewed the gas turbine with reluctance and failed to make any constructive decisions for Bristol involvement until it was almost too late for the Company to join in the gas turbine race. By the middle of 1942, the gas turbine was sufficiently advanced for most people in the aircraft engine business to know that it could well be the engine of the future. The long struggle by Frank Whittle for official recognition, which ended in 1939 with a contract for an engine from his company, Power Jets Limited, and the construction of an aircraft by the Gloster Company was vindicated when that aeroplane flew successfully on 15 May 1941 using Whittle's engine. There followed the usual British mixture of bureaucracy and industrial inefficiency which in November 1942 led a young engineer, Stanley Hooker of Rolls-Royce to get his company interested in jet propulsion. Meanwhile, in Germany, the prototype of the Messerschmit 262 was flying with two Junkers jets. Germany was the first nation to get a gas turbine into the air using the Heinkel 178 which made the world's first jet flight on 27 August 1939, four days before Hitler's invasion of Poland. Fedden was reasonably well aware of these achievements, but remained curiously uninterested in jet propulsion. He did however express interest in the turbo-prop, a gas turbine driving a propeller rather than relying purely on reaction propulsion.

Work was underway on design studies at Patchway by the beginning of 1941 under the direction of Frank Owner. The development of the turbo jet, later to be named Theseus, proceeded in parallel with the big new radial, the Orion. Throughout 1941 relationships between Fedden and the Board deteriorated. Fedden, for his part, suspected that the Board planned to replace him with Norman Rowbotham, the successful manager of the Accrington plant, and the Board were deeply concerned about Fedden's lack of financial control.

Fedden was knighted in the New Year's Honours List of 1942. His official biographer states that this well merited honour came as a surprise to the Bristol Board and was resented by many of them. To anyone who knew the individuals involved, it comes as some surprise that this should be offered as one of the reasons for Fedden's departure from Bristol. The true reasons were more practical. Many years later Sir Reginald Verdon-Smith in a conversation with the present author outlined the situation very clearly. Fedden, in Sir Reginald's view, required strong leadership on the financial side. He involved Bristol Aeroplane Company in many serious difficulties, largely from giving over-optimistic programmes and greatly exceeding cost estimates. He shared the limitations of Brunel in that both men could set no limits to their imaginations. In engineering, it is necessary to let a project settle down and be produced in saleable quantities before modifications are introduced. Fedden was very much a driver of men, forcing ideas from them around the clock every day of the year. It is not surprising that the organisation failed to absorb all the ideas, and that when this happened Fedden felt frustrated and let down.

Matters came to a head on 1 October 1942 when Sir William Verdon-Smith instructed Fedden to leave the Bristol premises. He was succeeded by Norman Rowbotham.

Production of the vast quantities of Bristol engines continued uninterrupted by Fedden's departure but the disruption in the design team was soon apparent. Prominent figures left. Butler died of a heart attack, largely through overwork, and the engine division began a period of various misfortunes which were not to abate until the arrival of Stanley Hooker six years later. Nevertheless, in the Centaurus Bristol had probably the best radial engine in the world and the design studies for the Theseus were going ahead. The Orion would be dropped, but Frank Owner had the Theseus running just before the end of the Japanese war on 18 July 1945. In the meanwhile he had begun work on the 4000 h.p. engine named the Proteus, another gas turbo-prop which was planned for use in the immense Brabazon airliner by now taking shape in No. 2 Flight Shed at Filton.

This huge machine, together with the Brigand, the tail end of the Buckmaster and the Freighter were the products that the Bristol Aeroplane Company were offering for the first years of peace. It had been a long war and one can forgive the employees at Filton if they relaxed for a while and considered the achievements of the factories during the war years. The total output of aeroplanes from the factories in the U.K. from 3 September 1939 to 15 August 1945 was 10,733 machines, 3672 Blenheims, 1377 Beauforts, 20 Bombays, 5557 Beaufighters, 30 Buckinghams, 24 Buckmasters and two Brigands. The total also included 50 Hawker Tempest Mark 11s which were produced at the Banwell factory. For the record it should be noted that 676 Bolingbrokes were produced by Fairchild Aircraft Limited at their Longueuil factory in Quebec, Canada, and in Australia, 746 Beauforts and 364 Beaufighters were produced. To this tremendous achievement in aircraft production must be added the figures of Bristol engines. It is appropriate that the composition of the Board of the Bristol Aeroplane Company which led these achievements should be recorded as a final comment on the Second World War. The Chairman was Sir William Verdon-Smith, C.B.E.; Managing Director Sir Stanley White, Bart.; H. J. Thomas; George S. M. White; W. Reginald Verdon-Smith; N. Rowbotham; Captain K.G.J. Bartlett and J. S. Daniel.

The Filton and Patchway factories closed for victory celebrations on 8 and 9 May and again for the celebrations of the victory over Japan on 15 and 16 August. As the factories returned to work, plans were soon put in hand to meet the impending reduction in orders for military equipment and to obtain work for the troubled years of peace that lay ahead.

6

Britannia's Uncertain Rule

1945 – 1960

*'These great programmes needed many courageous decisions on
his part. Lesser men would have wilted under the responsibility
he bore during the Britannia crisis ... Only the cool courage
of Verdon kept the company afloat.'*

Sir Stanley Hooker on Sir Reginald Verdon-Smith in
Not Much of an Engineer, his autobiography.

Nothing demonstrated the transfer from war to peace more dramatically than events at the Oldmixon Shadow Factory at Weston-super-Mare during the summer of 1945. When the last Beaufighter came off the production line, the factory immediately commenced its next project for the Ministry of Supply: not aeroplanes but houses. Aircraft techniques and light alloy materials lent themselves to the rapid construction of pre-fabricated homes. Enemy bombing and the suspension of domestic house building for six years had led to desperate shortages, and these single-storey houses, made up mostly of light alloy sections and sheets, were a godsend. With a hall, living room, two bedrooms, bathroom and toilet and a fully equipped kitchen, they needed sites of only 30ft by 22.5ft. They found a ready market with local authorities nationwide. Pre-fabricated school buildings and hospitals, too, were erected. This activity continued through most of the '40s and some of the Company's houses are still standing today, fifty years later.

Another sign of peace in the air was the return of No. 501 (County of Gloucester) Squadron to Filton. Heavily involved in the Battle of Britain, operating from stations as diverse as Croydon and Middle Wallop, it returned to Filton for Christmas 1940 but left again in April the following year, by which time it had re-equipped with Spitfire 11s. These were followed by Spitfire Vs in 1942 and eventually as the war progressed, the Squadron was re-equipped again, this time with the Hawker Tempest Mark V, flying in operations against the German flying bombs, the notorious V1s. Stood down from wartime activity on 30 April 1945, the Squadron was reformed at Filton on 10 May 1946, and later that year received Spitfire 16s. These were replaced with Vampire jetfighters in February 1949 and these little twin-boom aircraft became a familiar sight exercising over north Bristol and the surrounding Gloucestershire countryside.

The decision to scrap the Royal Auxiliary Air Force in the early months of 1957 was not popular in Bristol but the Squadron stood down at a final parade held at Filton on 2 February 1957. It was still flying Vampire Vs and a tragic accident occurred at the time of the stand down proceedings. One of the Squadron pilots, in protest against the dissolution of the Squadron, made an unauthorised flight under the Clifton Suspension Bridge but failed to make the turn to climb out of the Gorge and crashed into the southern side of the River Avon. It was a spectacular but tragic end to an impressive record of Bristol's own R.A.F. Squadron.

Elsewhere in the City, B.O.A.C. left Whitchurch in 1945 and their very large hangars and overhaul facilities were immediately taken over by the Bristol Aeroplane Company's aero-engine division, for a large repair base for jet engines. The Bristol and Wessex Aeroplane Club was reformed but private flying, which had been banned during the war, did not start up until the spring of 1946. Great Western and Southern Airlines re-opened the Bristol-Cardiff service during the winter of 1946 but when the airline was taken into the new B.E.A. (British European Airways) in February 1947, the service was abruptly ended. Another operator at Whitchurch was Cambrian Airways, which operated De Havilland Rapides, Herons and Doves and also the Douglas DC3. Services extended to the Channel Islands, Southampton and the Isle of Man and a significant boost to services occurred on 3 May 1951 when Aer Lingus recommenced the Bristol to Dublin service.

The expansion of Bristol, even using some of the Bristol Aeroplane Company's pre-fabs, soon began to force the Airport Committee to consider a more flexible site than that provided by the old Whitchurch Airport. Large housing estates were springing up all around and in 1954 the City Council purchased the disused R.A.F. field at Lulsgate Bottom. Following the construction of a new terminal building and repairs to the runways, the new airport was opened by Her Royal Highness Princess Marina, Duchess of Kent, on 1 May 1957. A runway extension followed in 1963 and there have been continual improvements to the terminal building over the years. Bristol Airport became well established as a provincial airport.

Around Bristol, the many small sub-contractors who had undertaken war work for the Company had lost their contracts but not before some of them had established themselves as viable Bristol engineering businesses. Among the long established companies, Parnalls remained in business after the war and were major sub-contractors during the Britannia Project, undertaking large components for the aircraft production assembly line at Filton.

The Bristol Aeroplane Company entered 1946 with confidence. Three developments would dominate the Board's deliberations. The Board were committed to the development of a giant commercial airliner. Secondly, a decision was made to enter the helicopter market. The design and building of helicopters were to remain part of the Company's activities until the formation of the British Aircraft Corporation in 1960 and just beyond. The third consideration was the civil market for which the Company had an excellent project on offer, the Type 170 Freighter/Wayfarer which was begining to attract orders in some numbers. Then in December 1946, the state airline B.O.A.C. issued a specification for a Medium Range Empire transport. The machine required was almost identical to an uprated Lockheed Constellation which Bristol proposed to build under licence at Filton. This bold venture, which might have had considerable consequences for the British aircraft industry, getting under the American belt, as it were, at an early stage, was banned by the Treasury under Sir Stafford Cripps who would not allow the necessary dollars to be invested in the American company to enable the Filton project to go ahead. Nevertheless it excited Bristol interest in medium size transports, leading to the eventual order for the Britannia airliner and consequently to one of the most difficult periods of the Company's history.

Of these aircraft, the Wayfarer was the simplest, in design, philosophy and structure. After Russell's design team had rejected the possiblity of using Buckingham components to turn out a light freighter, the resultant aircraft owes far more to the Bombay than any other previous Bristol design. The Freighter Wayfarer emerged as one of the ugliest aircraft flying at the time, but as it developed it attracted a certain grace. It had a wing span of 98 feet which was eventually stretched to 108 feet in later variants. It was never able to do better than 163 miles per hour and possessed a maximum range, again in the later marks, of 900 miles. However, for any operator who wished to carry unconventional loads at a reasonable cost, it was certainly an attractive aeroplane. It first flew on 2 December 1945 in the safe hands of Captain Uwins. This was the last prototype that 'CFU' flew for the Company before his retirement as Chief Test Pilot in 1947. No one had tested more prototypes with such safety and skilful airmanship and his record remains unequalled in the British aircraft industry. Captain Uwins also achieved the distinction of being one of the first 'non-family' directors of the Bristol Aeroplane Company.

The Freighter was assembled at the Filton Works in the Erecting Hall at the top of Filton Hill. It was the last aircraft to be fully assembled there less the outer wings and was then towed down hill to the Flight Sheds where the wings were attached. It says something for the speed of work and the confidence at Bristol that the third prototype Freighter, having first flown on 23 June 1946, set out on 3 August for a demonstration tour of both North and South America. It crossed the Atlantic by way of Iceland, Greenland and Newfoundland and arrived in Toronto. From there it traversed the Americas, going as far south as Buenos Aires, crossing the Andes to Chile and then all the way back to the United States. Here it was chartered to various operators and eventually arrived back at Filton in March 1948 where it became

Initial stages of assembly of a Bristol Freighter in 1948.

Assembling engines and nose-loading doors to a Freighter.

A Bristol Freighter being fitted out in the Erecting Hall in 1949.

Bristol Type 170 Freighter Mk. 31 (108ft span, 2 x 1980hp Hercules 734, 240 mph max.)
of the RNZAF flying over north-west Bristol.

*The first stretched version of the Freighter on flight from Filton in 1952. The extra length
allowed a third saloon car to be carried. 214 of all marks of Freighter were built.*

the first machine to operate the Trans-Channel Car Ferry set up by Silver City Airways. This car ferry service was to develop into big business in the 1950s and Dr Russell especially stretched the Freighter in the nose and on the wing tips in order to get a third car into the hull. The Freighter sold all around the world, two squadrons going to the Royal Pakistan Airforce and versions appearing in Spain, New Zealand and South America. In all, Filton produced 214 of these very useful aeroplanes by the time production ceased in March 1958.

The last Freighter, the Mark 32, was undoubtedly the best known version and was a familiar sight over the English Channel in the livery of Silver City Airways which became British United Air Ferries in October 1962. These aircraft did an incredible number of landings, three at least making the 25,000 landing mark without any problem.

The early Freighters were not without their problems and led to two of the three fatal accidents suffered by Filton-based company aircraft since the Second World War. On 6 May 1949, Freighter G-AIFF took off on what was thought to be a routine test flight. The aircraft was flown by Dickie Northway with several test engineers on board for a series of one engine climbs. About an hour later, the aircraft was seen by one of Her Majesty's submarines cruising on the surface, to plunge into the sea off Portland Bill with the loss of the entire crew. Attempts at salvage proved impossible and the cause of the disaster remained a mystery. The problem was solved, again tragically, when another Freighter crashed on 21 March 1950 in South Wales. The cause was considered to be structural failure of the fin. Modkits were immediately produced in an emergency programme in the factory to fit a dorsal fin to all freighters and thus the problem was solved. A further part of the modification entailed placing stops at the base of the rudder post with a transverse arm which prevented the rudder going into the extreme yaw position and a state of flutter. These problems apart, the Freighter proved a successful and useful money spinner for the Company during the difficult post-war years.

Meanwhile, the giant Bristol Brabazon I, allocated the Company's type number 167, was taking shape. The story of the Brabazon is one of the most remarkable in the Bristol or any company's history and it remains one of the largest aircraft ever built. The origins of the Brabazon design can be traced back to 1942 when the Company was asked to submit a design study for a very large bomber using four Centaurus or six Hercules engines and weighing as much as 100,000 lbs. This was very much on the limits of size that could be accommodated by contemporary technology and in order to utilise the power available effectively, it was necessary to cut down wherever possible. Thus the idea was conceived of burying the engines inside the wings. Once committed to this particular train of thought, Leslie Frise and Russell extrapolated the initial design study until they had produced a very large monoplane, using eight Centaurus and a weight of 22,500 lbs. This design never got a Bristol type number and is usually known as the Hundred-Ton Bomber. In many ways it was a remarkable machine but by 1943 the Royal Air Force preferred to increase its orders for Lancasters, a proven machine, and military interest in the Hundred-Ton Bomber lapsed.

Coincidentally with this bomber design, the Ministry of Aircraft Production had been investigating the possibilities for British civil airliner production after the war. Beaverbrook, who had just retired as Minister of Aircraft Production, was fully aware that the Americans now had a strangle-hold on civil airliner design and production, and therefore a meeting was called of a number of British designers. Bristol was not included in this august assembly and this produced a quite justified protest from Leslie Frise. In the event, he produced the design study for a long-range British transport and this happened to coincide with the report of a Cabinet Committee under Lord Brabazon which recommended to the Government the types of aircraft which in its judgement would meet the needs of the civil market following the war. On 11 March 1943, the Secretary of State for Air announced in the House of Commons that a contract for producing the first of these recommendations of the Brabazon Committee had been awarded to the Bristol Aeroplane Company. The aircraft was immediately named Brabazon Mark I and its design and assembly went ahead on the strict condition that it would not interfere with the Company's programmes of military work. On 29 May the Ministry announced that it had ordered two prototypes with ten more production aircraft in view. Various requirements such as passenger space and comfort, range and power led to a design which called for a wing span of 230 feet and a length of 177 feet. It was the largest airliner ever conceived anywhere in the world.

By the time the huge machine was beginning to take shape, the Bristol factory was to lose the services of its Chief Engineer, the gifted protegé of Barnwell, Leslie Frise. He had been made Chief Engineer

The Brabazon Assembly Hall under construction in 1946.

following the death of Barnwell in 1938 and had played a key role in the development of the Company's twin-engined military aircraft designs which were its major contribution to the national war effort. As the war ended, he was deeply involved in the Brabazon project.

All was not well, however. Sir Archibald Russell relates in his autobiography that, when the dispersed design team returned to Filton to occupy the newly-built design office (an art-deco apparition immediately tagged 'The Odeon'), Sir Stanley White insisted that Frise move instead to Filton House. The same tactic had been used before when closer supervision of Barnwell had been considered by the Board to be desirable.

Frise for some reason had long standing grievances about the Board and told Russell that 'they had the skids under me'. In any event, in 1946 Leslie Frise left Filton to join Hunting Aviation as Technical Director. Russell succeeded him as Chief Engineer.

In any consideration of the Brabazon project, it must borne in mind that its proposers were drawing on their experience of aviation in the 1930s. This form of travel was a luxurious and expensive process. Aeroplanes were comfortable, flew at low altitudes and the standard of service on board was excellent. All the potatoes were peeled and cooked in the galley, the food was served piping hot, it was possible to 'promenade' on an Empire Flying Boat and the process was certainly leisurely by today's standards. The initial design of the Brabazon Airliner included a separate dining room although this had to be discarded when a 25 ft diameter fuselage was found to induce too much drag. Nevertheless this large aeroplane was schemed for 70 passengers in sleeping berths.

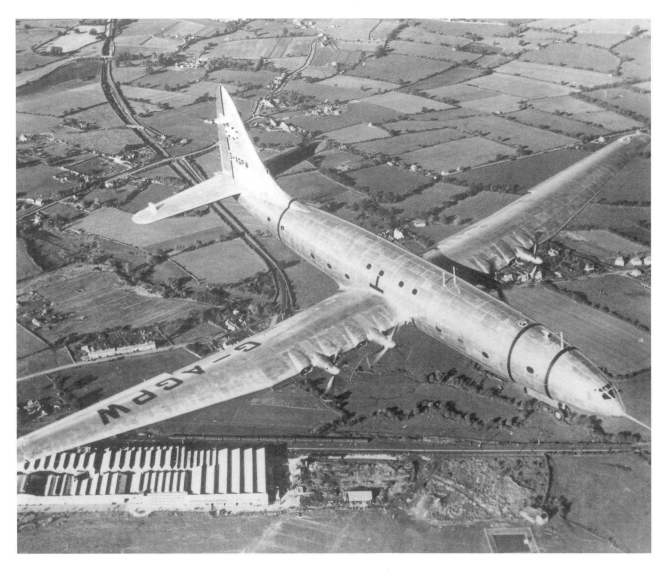

The giant Bristol Brabazon I in flight over Patchway in 1950.

The completed Assembly Hall which has given over half a century of continuous service.

The main features of the design had been finalised by the end of 1944 and the first drawings went out to the workshops in April of 1945. By this time the designers had already solved one of their major problems, albeit at heavy cost to a small Gloucestershire community. First plans were to build the Brabazon at the Oldmixon factory at Weston-Super-Mare, where the runway was considerably longer than that at Filton. However the sandy soil of the Somerset plain proved unequal to taking the weight of the aircraft without considerable civil engineering work. A decision was therefore taken to extend the runway at Filton in a westerly direction towards the River Severn. The small hamlet of Charlton lay in the way as did a new Bristol by-pass road, then one of the few dual carriageways in the country. Government approval for the village's demolition was given, and today it is just a fond memoy from a by-gone age.

In addition to a large, long and strong runway, accommodation had to be found for the new giant aircraft. This was done by building a new three-bay hangar on an 8 acre site south of the Filton to Avonmouth railway and with a level crossing with automatically controlled gates to allow the aircraft to pass out to the airfield. This hangar was at the time the largest aircraft assembly hall in Europe and possibly in the world. It was designed by the Bristol Aeroplane Company's architect, Eric Ross, but only one bay was ready for the Brabazon when it was moved out of Number 2 Flight Shed into its final erection position in the Assembly Hall (East Bay) on 4 October 1947.

Completion of the aircraft then went ahead rapidly. Flight tests on such aircraft as Lancasters and Buckmasters were carried out for various new components of the Brabazon. As Archibald Russell said later, 'we had new engine couplings, new hydraulics, new power flying controls and new air-conditioning techniques. You can't get much more new than that.' The aircraft was completed in December 1948 when the Company held the first of those 'roll-out' ceremonies which are a familiar feature of today's aircraft industry. The Brabazon roll-out ceremony was significant for the emergence of two personalities who would take significant rôles in the history of Bristol aviation in the immediate future. The roll-out ceremony was performed by Air Chief Marshal Sir Alec Coryton, the Controller of Equipment at the Ministry. In charge of the ceremony for the Company on that day was Sir William Verdon-Smith's son, Mr W. Reginald Verdon-Smith who was taking at this time an increasingly important rôle in the affairs of the Company.

Bristol would see much of Sir Alec in the years that lay ahead. He had already a distinguished career in the R.A.F. behind him and a reputation for concern for the safety of his aircrews while commanding a bomber group under 'Bomber' Harris. When he left the Ministry of Supply in mid-1951, Sir Alec Coryton was appointed Managing Director of the Bristol Engine Division and would provide badly needed leadership at a time of crisis. Reginald Verdon-Smith was born in 1912 and educated at Repton and Brasenose College, Oxford where he took a first in law. On leaving university in 1938, he joined the Company and became a director in 1942. Just thirty, he carried responsibility for the Company's shadow factories for much of the war. Now, in 1949 he was Joint Assistant Managing Director. Courteous and urbane but always decisive, he was on the threshold of a brilliant career which would make him one of the foremost industrialists and financiers in Great Britain.

The roll-out ceremony over, work now proceeded to ready the first prototype for flight, an event much delayed by the demolition of Charlton and the severe winter of 1947 which delayed runway and hangar completion. Already in 1946 it had been agreed by the Ministry of Supply that the first aeroplane would be completed as a non-passenger research aircraft. It would be powered by eight Centaurus XX engines, coupled in pairs and driving contra-rotating airscrews by Rotol. The second machine would be equipped to carry 100 passengers and be powered by a coupled version of the new Proteus turbo-prop which Frank Owner had under development at Patchway. Only a few people realised that the Proteus carried the whole future of the Bristol Aeroplane Company in its unorthodox design.

The Bristol Brabazon Mark 1 first flew at 1130 hours Sunday, 4 September 1949, in the safe hands of Bill Pegg. To the many thousands who were present, the event remains one of majestic memory. The great silver aircraft proceeded – there can be no other word – into the sunny autumn sky with an inevitable authority. Pegg, with Walter Gibb as co-pilot, flew an uneventful circuit of the south Gloucestershire countryside and then returned to a triumphant landing at Filton and the plaudits of the world's press corps who had been waiting in hordes at Filton for several days.

To the British, suffering the austerity of the early post-war years, the Brabazon was a sign of long awaited national recovery and Pegg was accorded the fame usually reserved for royalty and Hollywood stars. To most of those closely involved with the project, the aircraft remains the most impressive of their careers and their Brabazon memories would fill several volumes.

During 1949 to 1951, the Brabazon was a familiar sight in the sky over Bristol. Its approach was heralded by the heavy droning note of its eight engines and people would emerge in hundreds to watch the leviathan go by. At Filton, however, and in the offices of the Ministry of Supply and B.O.A.C., the doubts were already accumulating. The aircraft had been designed to a specification more suited to the thirties than the fifties and for passengers who had been equally at home in the lounges of the *Queen Mary* and *Normandie* or the hull of an Empire flying-boat. Such a market no longer existed, and to rub the point home, the vacant third bay of the Assembly Hall at Filton had been leased temporarily to B.O.A.C.'s Atlantic Division while Heathrow (London) Airport was being constructed. The aircraft accommodated were Boeing Stratocruisers and Lockheed Constellations, profitable post-war derivatives of American military production, each of which could outperform the Brabazon in speed and payload (but not range) at about a third of the aircraft cost.

With less than 400 hours flown, multiple fatigue cracks began to appear in the airscrew mounting structures and, while not fatal in themselves, they led to forecasts of an airframe life of only 5000 flying hours. Work on the project was suspended in February 1952, the contract cancelled in September of that year and both airframes (the second one-third complete) broken up in October 1953.

Fifty years on, it is tempting to hail the Brabazon as the forerunner of today's wide-bodied jet airliners. This is to falsify history, as the whole scheme was an example of how not to construct a modern aircraft. Schemed by a Government committee who failed to consult the airlines and funded by ever available state money, the project cost the taxpayer dear. On the positive side, the Assembly Hall has served successive Filton projects well and the 8000-foot runway could one day become the base of a new airport north of Bristol. In the meanwhile, those who had the good fortune to work on the Brabazon will recollect those heady days of 1949 with nostalgic pride.

The failure of the Brabazon to enter series production made little impact on the immediate employment situation at Filton. Freighter Type 170 production continued in the Erecting Hall, series production of the Type 171 helicopter and Type 173 prototype was in full swing in the Flight Sheds, the new Car Division was scoring triumphs on the international racing circuits and a deal with Ferranti in 1949 to

Bristol Type 175 Britannia 102 (142ft 3in span, 4 x 2800hp Proteus 625, 362 mph cruise)
G-ANBA, the first production Britannia, flying over Bristol in 1955.

The first Britannia 102s come off the production line in the Assembly Hall in the autumn of 1955.

produce surface-to-air guided missiles had seen the birth of the Bristol missile business. A start had also been made in aircraft materials from plastics and glass fibre which would lead to lucrative orders in the late fifties for drop tanks and not-so profitable attempts to build car bodies for Lotus and high performance sailing dinghies.

All these diverse projects gave the Company what appeared on the surface to be a commercial base of some strength. In addition, the centre bay of the Assembly Hall was already laid out for production of Bristol Type 175, a four-engined medium range airliner to a specification from B.O.A.C., who had already given it the name Britannia. The production version was to be powered by the new Bristol Proteus turbo-prop engine, which, as we have seen, had been under development in a twin version for the Brabazon II and the Saro Princess flying boat.

The origins of the Britannia go back to 1943 when the Brabazon committee proposed a similar machine to compete with the Lockheed Constellation which was already in the air as a military transport. Little came of the proposal until December 1946 when B.O.A.C. issued a specification for their Medium Range Empire (MRE) airliner. In a realistic approach which would have had remarkable consequences, the Bristol Board suggested that a licence-built Constellation fitted with Centaurus engines would be the best solution. This imaginative plan was banned by the Attlee Government on the grounds of dollar expenditure. Specification 2/47 was then issued from which the Type 175 derived and an order for three prototypes was confirmed by the Ministry of Supply on 5 July 1948. Then, largely due to the interest of B.O.A.C., the Centaurus was replaced by the turbo-jet Proteus and the order reduced to two aircraft. Work went ahead speedily and with few snags, so good was Russell's basic design. In due course, B.O.A.C. signed a production order for 25 aircraft on 28 July 1949 for entry into service in 1954.

With Bill Pegg at the controls, the first Britannia G-ALBO flew at Filton on 16 August 1952 and such progress was made that it flew at the SBAC show at Farnborough in September. Thereafter, only two big modifications were needed – a revised jet pipe layout to exhaust gases clear of the nacelle and extended upturned wing tips to improve lateral stability.

The men who created the Britannia. Archibald E.(Russ) Russell (1904-96), left, Chief Engineer of the Aircraft Division, and Dr Stanley G. Hooker (1907-84), Technical Director of Bristol Engines, on the tarmac at Filton in the fifties. Both were outstanding figures in the industry and both would be knighted in due course among many other honours.

All this success concealed a critical struggle at Patchway to produce the Proteus engine to specification and on time. By early 1949 the sophisticated turbo-prop was in trouble on all fronts. Then it was that fate took a hand in the affairs at Patchway and bestowed new and dynamic leadership on the troubled plant. Out of the blue, Reginald Verdon-Smith received a telephone call from a friend of Oxford days, Stanley Hooker, who had achieved great things at Rolls-Royce under the tutelage of that company's great Chairman, Lord Hives. Hooker had quarrelled with Hives over promotion and was looking for a fresh start. The two men met in London and it was agreed that Hooker would start at Bristol on 3 January 1949.

Stanley George Hooker was born on 30 September 1907 and studied aeronautics at Imperial College. After a short spell with the Admiralty, Hooker joined Rolls-Royce at Derby in 1938 and rose rapidly through that organisation, although he had no previous experience of aircraft engines. Hives gave Hooker his head at Rolls and within months Hooker had added thirty per cent more power to the crucially important Merlin engine. Then he had been entrusted with the task of developing Whittle's embryonic gas turbines into production engines. In a magical two years, Hooker increased the thrust of his jet engines from 1800 to 3000 lb. Throughout these years, Verdon-Smith had watched Hooker's progress from afar. No one new better how far Bristol lagged in jet practice and he saw in Hooker a great opportunity to rescue the Proteus and thereby the whole Britannia project.

Hooker found the whole ethos at Patchway still concentrated on piston engines, led by the Managing Director Norman Rowbotham. Against this, the Chief Engineer, Frank Owner, fought an uphill battle to develop jets. He told Hooker of the Proteus 'I decided to make the engine with the lowest fuel consumption in the world, regardless of weight and bulk. So far we have achieved the weight and bulk.'

In mid-1950, Verdon-Smith appointed Hooker to Chief Engineer of the Engine Division with full engineering authority. Owner left soon after to join De Havilland Engines and Hooker proceeded to a complete re-design of the Proteus. The outcome was the Proteus 700 series, half a ton lighter, a third of a metre shorter and much more fuel efficient than its predecessor. Power was increased from

A Filton visit by Sir Miles Thomas, Chairman of B.O.A.C. Sir Reginald Verdon-Smith and Cyril Uwins are left and right of the picture. Relations between Bristol and B.O.A.C. were not happy at the time in the mid-fifties.

The second Britannia prototype seen after crash landing in the Severn Estuary on 4 February 1954, due to a fractured reduction gear in the starboard inner engine. All on board were uninjured but the programme suffered a severe set back.

Sir Stanley White, Managing Director, hosts a visit of R.A.F. and U.S.A.F. officers to Filton in the fifties. Captain Cyril Uwins is first left in the second row and Sir George White, the second baronet, is fifth in the same row. A.J. 'Bill' Pegg, Chief Test Pilot, is far right in the back row.

Captain Cyril Uwins, third from right, front row, heads a group of Filton management in the sixties.
Frank Chard is third from the left and R.S. 'Bob' Brown far right, front row.

2500 to an eventual 4445 ehp and this engine would go into the production Britannia. One basic snag remained however. The cancellation of the Brabazon and the Princess aircraft came too late for Hooker to change the reverse-flow layout and this would cause trouble later.

Meanwhile, Britannia production was in full swing at Filton, with R.S. (Bob) Brown as General Manager and Frank Chard responsible for day-to-day control as Production Manager. Bristol appeared to have a world-beating aeroplane on its hands and interest from airlines was intense. Then disaster struck. On a demonstration flight the second prototype Britannia G-ALRX took off from Filton on 4 February 1954 with Pegg at the controls and Hooker and Dr Russell on board. High over Herefordshire, a reduction gear failure (the only part Hooker did not redesign) failed in the starboard inner engine, leading to an intense engine fire. Pegg set course for Filton but in the event decided to ditch on the broad, inviting mud banks of the Severn near Littleton. In this, by superb airmanship, he was successful, thereby saving the lives of all on board but the aircraft was a complete write-off. Hooker and his team soon redesigned the offending set of gears, but in May of the same year, the other prototype G-ALBO, flown by Walter Gibb, did a spectacular half-roll, following the fracture of a flap torque tube. Before Gibb could regain control, no easy task, 3g had been pulled on the airframe, which was grounded for full inspection. The flap tube was found to be made of incorrect material but this left the project with no airworthy machine and delays to the delivery programme ensued.

Hence it was not until December 1955 that two Series 102 machines were named to B.O.A.C. with full C. of A. certificates. In the meantime, a second production line had been set up at the Short plant in Belfast and an important licence agreement with Canadair in 1954 led to the eventual success of the CL28 and CL44, of which 72 would be built.

Now the way seemed clear for Britannia. Then, in March 1956, a Britannia 102 on final tropical clearance experienced flame-out on all four engines in extremely rare cloud conditions over Uganda. The

A sectioned Bristol Proteus in the Rolls-Royce Heritage collection, which clearly shows the reverse flow which caused so much trouble in Britannia days.

reason was build up of ice in the bends of the reverse-flow Proteus and Hooker quickly devised glow plugs to immediately re-light the engine in such conditions. B.O.A.C. however refused to accept the aircraft and two frustrating years followed while stocks of aircraft piled up with no delivery income. This caused a cash flow crisis which almost bankrupted the Bristol Company. Only the cool leadership of Reginald Verdon-Smith stood between it and disaster, but world airlines lost interest as a result. Eventually, the Israeli airline El Al bought three Series 313 long range aircraft and flew one non-stop from New York to Tel Aviv on 19 December 1957. This success did something to allay the gloom at Filton caused by the tragic crash of the Series 301 G-ANCA on 6 November 1957 at Downend, Bristol, killing all fifteen crew and test observers on board.

In all, 83 Britannias were eventually built, just sufficient to save the Bristol Aeroplane Company, according to Stanley Hooker. In the years that followed, the aircraft and its Proteus engines gave impeccable service but the stubborn attitude of B.O.A.C. over the development problems, following the demise of the Comet I, left the world airliner market open to Boeing and its Type 707. This attitude also led to the cancellation of the Orion, a superb turbo-prop which had much better power than the Proteus. Hooker and his team had this engine flying in a Britannia by August 1956 but Treasury insistence on only one new turbo-prop project led to cancellation in 1958 in preference to the Rolls-Royce type.

Reginald Verdon-Smith was knighted in 1958 and succeeded his father, Sir William, as Chairman of the Bristol Aeroplane Company two years later. The latter had served as Chairman since 1928.

By 1955, British aviation was moving into a period of drastic change. No fewer than 27 airframe and 8 engine plants competed in what was now a declining market. Even before the cataclysmic Duncan Sandys White Paper of 1957, it was clear that amalgamation was coming and the correct choice of partner was crucial to survival. Sir Reginald guided the reorganisation of the Bristol Companies into a structure in keeping with the new challenges. In January 1956, three new and separate companies were formed. Bristol Aircraft Ltd., Bristol Aero-Engines Ltd., and Bristol Cars Ltd. Chaired respectively by Cyril Uwins, Sir Alec Coryton and George White, each would eventually become partners in large new organisations. Bristol Aero-Engines amalgamated with Armstrong Siddeley Motors Ltd. to form Bristol Siddeley Engines Ltd. in April 1959 while Bristol Aircraft joined British Aircraft Corporation in partnership with Vickers and English Electric in June 1960. Since February 1910, 15,750 aircraft of 85 different designs had been built at Filton or in plants under its direct control while 8320 licence-built machines brought the total to 25,070 aircraft in fifty years. Now the Bristol plant became the Filton Division of British Aircraft Corporation and a new era began.

7

DIVERSIONS

1945 – 1960

'Memory seems restricted to the many "fixed wing" aeroplanes (Bristol) produced; seldom ever is mention made of their helicopters.'

C.T.D. (Sox) Hosegood-Chief Test Pilot, Bristol Helicopters.

'We cannot afford to disregard the clear indications towards progress offered by the rotative wing.'

Raoul Hafner to the Royal Aeronautical Society, October 1937.

While the difficulties surrounding the Britannia project were the major preoccupation of the Bristol Aeroplane Company in the years after the Second World War, it nevertheless took every opportunity to enter new fields of aviation that promised a commercial return. The forties saw the start of projects to construct helicopters and guided missiles, while a major investment was made in the production of automobiles. With the roots of the firm originating in the tram and bus industry, and Fedden's constant proposals for car designs, the decision to build cars came as no surprise. Helicopters were a different matter.

Today, the helicopter is a familiar sight and its useful versatility well known to the general public. Yet the helicopter arrived late on the aviation scene. The principle of deriving lift from a bladed rotor had been known since the days of Leonardo da Vinci but success with full size machines was elusive, due to the mechanics of rotor power and control, and the problems with subsequent torque. During the twenties and thirties, Cierva and Hafner in Great Britain and Igor Sikorsky in the U.S.A. all enjoyed increasing degrees of success. In particular, Sikorsky invented the anti-torque tail rotor which was the key to practical helicopter operation. This coincided with the outbreak of the war in 1939. The early Sikorsky military machines raised considerable interest in Europe and a number of companies decided to enter the helicopter field. Among these were Westland, licence-building Sikorsky designs, Cierva, Fairey and Bristol.

Bristol began to form its helicopter department in the autumn of 1944 and it offered the post of Chief Designer (Helicopters) to Raoul Hafner, at the same time taking over the assets, manufacturing rights and patents of Hafner's AR III (Hafner Gyroplane) Company. A number of his colleagues joined Hafner, first at the Weston factory in October and then moved to Filton in June 1945.

Hafner was already a famous name in the helicopter world. A native of Austria, he built and flew his first single-seat helicopter in Vienna in 1930. He moved to England in 1932, bringing his second machine with him and opened his own company at Feltham, where he produced his third machine, a successful autogiro, the AR III. Hafner became a British citizen in September 1940 after a short period of internment and then spent the war years experimenting with troop-carrying rotorcraft. These consisted of free-fall rotors, supporting one soldier and a Bren gun and later (in 1943) developed into sufficient size to support the weight of a standard jeep. In the event, the Allies solved these problems with the use of parachutes and gliders, and there was no opposition to Hafner's departure to Bristol.

At once, Hafner got down to the first design studies for a single rotor helicopter. This was designated the Bristol Type 171 and a search for a suitable powerplant began as nothing of appropriate size (550 h.p.)

The first Bristol venture into helicopters was the Type 171 Sycamore (48ft 7in rotor, 550hp Alvis Leonides, 132 mph) of which 181 were eventually built at Bristol and Weston. The aircraft shown is the company Mk 3 demonstrator.

The next Bristol helicopter, the Type 173 took a long, expensive time to develop. Pitch up in forward flight was one problem of many. Originally powered by two Leonides, these were replaced by Napier Gazelles and the aircraft renumbered Type 192 Belvedere but before 26 were built, Bristol helicopter interests had passed to Westland in February 1960.

was under development at Patchway. Eventually, the Alvis Leonides was chosen but because this engine was not yet cleared for series production, the first two prototypes flew with the American Pratt and Whitney Wasp Junior which power was slightly on the low side at 450 h.p.

The Type 171 was the first British commercial helicopter and took almost three years to design and develop to first flight. This lengthy process derived from the need to thoroughly test the advanced rotor head and blade design, which incorporated Hafner's tie-bar control concept and the ability to auto-rotate to a safe landing in the event of power failure. This entailed the construction of the first rotor test tower in the world, which rapidly became a local landmark, almost on the crest of Filton Hill adjacent to the golf course. It was 50 feet high to get above ground cushion effects and the rotor chattered busily for hours on end. Ground running began on 4 May 1947 and the first flight was carried out on 27 July by H.A. Marsh, an Air Registration Board pilot with helicopter experience. The co-pilot was Eric Swiss who would be later appointed the Chief Test Pilot for the project. The second aircraft flew in February of the following year and test flying went ahead. The first deliveries of the Alvis Leonides engines started in the summer of 1948 and this power plant was fitted to the prototype Mk. 2. A long period of engine type testing followed and the Mk. 2 did not get airborne until 3 September 1949, the day before the first flight of the Brabazon. Swiss piloted a smooth, short flight, then alighted and made to take off for a second ascent. Due to a poor clutch design, unacceptable acceleration was forced on the rotors and their wooden construction shattered into hundreds of small pieces. No injuries resulted and the problem was soon cured with a stronger rotor and revised clutch design.

The Mk.3 Sycamore, as the Type 171 was called by the R.A.F., was the production version and several versions were built. The type proved versatile although it never quite enjoyed the success of the early Westland helicopters. The best sales order was to the Federal German Government which ordered 50, deliveries beginning in 1955. Eventually 180 Sycamores were built, the last R.A.F. machine making its final flight on 11 August 1972.

Meanwhile, a second Bristol helicopter, designated the Type 173, was being designed and built. Offered in response to an Air Ministry requirement for a 8-10-seat machine, the 173 was to be Britain's first twin-engined helicopter and the first fore-and-aft twin-rotored helicopter.

During these years, the slight figure of Raoul Hafner, usually wearing a slouch hat that became his trade mark, was a familiar figure around the Filton shops. Ever approachable, he was easily diverted and would soon be delivering impromptu advice on rotary flight to an enthralled audience of apprentices. He became a popular and respected figure, much admired by the Filton workforce.

The Type 173 was designed and produced quickly, largely due to the proven worth of the Sycamore power plant and rotor, two of which Hafner now transferred into the 78-feet long 173. The rotor drives were interconnected by a drive shaft, so that if an engine failure occurred, both rotors continued to turn on one engine, although the main purpose of the drive was to obtain engine r.p.m. synchronisation and the aircraft could not sustain flight on one engine. Registered as G-ALBN, the machine made its first hovering flight on 3 January 1952 with Sox Hosegood at the controls. Earlier attempts had highlighted a major attitude problem of pitch up in forward flight, leading wags to quip 'we have a chopper that sits up and begs!' Despite persistent Filton legend that the machine would only fly backwards, Hosegood made no attempt at lateral flight in any direction although he did experience severe ground resonance and made repeated attempts to land before he at last coaxed G-ALBN to earth. Once this problem was eliminated (by mods to the rotor-hub gear and the undercarriage), another snag arose when the machine persisted in turning to starboard even when Hosegood had every control hard over to port. Rotor blade angles were adjusted and the angle of the tail fin changed and finally in August 1952 the Type 173 left the Filton control zone for its first short, flight.

The 173 was the subject of much service interest from both the Royal Navy and the R.A.F. The stream of modifications continued, the most prominent to the eye being the attempt to obtain lateral stability by several dramatic changes of design to the tail empennage. This started life as a severely up-swept tailplane, was replaced in the second prototype, the Mark 2, with large stub wings fore and aft until eventually the solution was found in a tailplane of modest size, set at anhedral and with small tip fins.

The Bristol Board supported Hafner and his team with surprising confidence, even though the helicopter venture had so far provided little profit. Sycamores were in production, however, and the prospects for the twin-engined machine remained quite encouraging. A decision was taken, therefore, to concentrate all helicopter activity at the Oldmixon factory at Weston-super-Mare, starting in March 1955 with the Sycamore production line. The 95th and subsequent Sycamores were assembled at Weston.

Work went ahead on twin rotor development, much of it funded by development contracts for the Bristol 191, a successor to the 173, of which only three ever flew. The 191 was a ship-borne anti-submarine helicopter for the Royal Navy and in April 1956, the Company got a contract for three prototypes and a staggering order for 65 production machines. At the same time, an order for the R.A.F. of a general purpose helicopter, the Bristol Type 192, was received In the 1957 Defence Review the 191 was cancelled, the engine and transmission problems of the Type 173 Mark 3 having much to do with the decision, although it was largely a political one. As a small palliative, and to keep twin rotor development in being, the order for the 192 was increased from 22 to 26!

The first flight of the prototype Type 192 took place on 5 July 1958 with Sox Hosegood again at the controls and Jack Hobbs as observer. The layout was similar to earlier Bristol designs but the great step forward was the powerplant installation of two Napier Gazelles, a gas turbine developed for helicopters with ability to operate at any attitude. The type first ran in December 1955 and after development, delivered a useful 1650bhp. Another improvement was the introduction of metal rotor blades. Metal blades were not ready for the first flight, although eventually all 192s received them.

The type 192 entered R.A.F. service at Odiham in August 1961 and was in active use for only seven years. The limitation of its naval-based design affected operational qualities and the airframe had a life of only 1600 hours. Nevertheless, it spent much time on active service in the Gulf and Malaya and, as the Belvedere, will be remembered as the last wholly Bristol-designed aircraft in squadron service with the R.A.F.

In February 1960, government policy dictated massive amalgamations of British aircraft and aero-engine manufacturers. This will be discussed in detail in the next chapter but among the decisions resulting from the policy was the concentration of all British helicopter design and manufacture under Westlands at Yeovil. Bristol Helicopters Ltd., now passed to Westlands. The Bristol designs, which included a large civil design – Type 194 – were abandoned and Hafner's design team dispersed. Hafner became Director of Research at Yeovil in 1962 and continued until his retirement in 1968 . He was to die tragically on 14 November 1980, aged seventy-five, when he was lost in the Bristol Channel with three companions in a freak storm which overwhelmed his yacht.

As for Bristol, the venture into helicopters was hardly an unqualified success although two of the three types reached production and 209 machines were built from 1947 to 1952. The watchful eyes of Reginald Verdon-Smith and William Masterton ensured that financial return was satisfactory but the failure to fully enter the civil market was disappointing.

The second of the three major ventures undertaken by the Bristol Aeroplane Company in the immediate post-war period was the decision to enter the high quality automobile market and to manufacture cars at Filton. The production of motorbus bodies had provided much needed work at Filton in the lean years following the First World War and the decision to make cars sprang in some measure from a similar desire to replace work losses. In 1942, at the height of the war, Fedden had a small team scheming a car of advanced design but this came to naught with Fedden's departure from the Company. The moving spirit in the car venture was George White, grandson of the founder and later to be third baronet. Born on 11 April 1913, he was educated at Harrow and Magdalene College, Cambridge and joined the Company on coming down from university. George White was to make the Bristol car a lifetime preoccupation and it is largely due to his determination that the Bristol marque has survived in production to this day.

Work at Filton was already underway by September 1945 and for the next decade and a half, the Bristol Aeroplane Company produced a series of Bristol models that were the equal of anything in their class world-wide. The emphasis was on hand-built quality and when the Bristol 400 appeared at the 1947 Geneva motor show, it made an immediate impact. *The Motor* magazine called it a 'car of exceptional ability' and the chassis design proved so good that it was used for all subsequent Bristol 2 and 2.2 litre models. The Bristol engine was a roaring success and the Company competed at Le Mans, while other versions of the engine were used by Cooper to power Grand Prix cars. The late Mike Hawthorn began his brilliant career with Bristols.

During the early fifties when the success of the Bristol Car Division was at its height, everyone on site at Filton took a proprietorial interest in the car enterprise and its fortunes. The heavy articulated vans which were the mobile support shops of the Bristol racing team were a familiar sight in the factory and their departure for an international event always attracted a supportive crowd. Then there was 'Mr George', always to be seen driving to his office in the latest Bristol saloon, often stopping for a word with employees along the route.

In 1956 the Car Division became Bristol Cars Ltd, with George White as Chairman. Already there was Government pressure for the major aircraft firms to amalgamate and in 1961, the Bristol Aeroplane Company became a part of British Aircraft Corporation. In this aircraft giant, there was no room for a small satellite making a handful of high quality cars and George White, with fellow director T.A.D. Crook, bought out Bristol Cars Ltd and went fully independent.

Although the cars continued to be made at Filton for a period, the production of Bristol engines ceased in 1961 and the next Bristol model was fitted with a 5 litre Chrysler V Eight! However, the car prospered and so has the Bristol marque, surviving on a careful policy of unostentatious quality motors for people with discernment and money. In 1967, George White (who succeeded to the baronetcy on the death of Sir Stanley in 1964) was badly hurt in a road accident when a new car on road test was in collision with a laundry van. He remained a director until his retirement due to ill health in 1973.

The third major initiative in the post-war years was a heavy investment in guided weapons. The Chinese were the first to use rockets in warfare many centuries ago and they were used in a fairly hit-or-miss fashion by the Royal Flying Corps against balloons in the 1914-18 war. A more sophisticated use of the weapon came

A Bristol 405 in 1955. Aircraft made good publicity backgrounds. The marque continues to be produced.

Among the earlier products of the Guided Weapons Division was the Bristol Ferranti Bloodhound Surface to Air missile seen here deployed on Britain's eastern coastline. Four rockets boosted the weapon into flight after which twin ram jets took over.

in 1943 when rockets were mounted on the Hawker Hurricane and they were in widespread use at the end of the war, the Hawker Typhoon proving itself a particularly steady rocket-launching platform. Rockets were also used in quantity by the Red Air Force in the Russian Campaign of 1941-45.

It was left to the Germans, however, to pioneer the first radio guidance systems fitted to weapons. The high casualty rate of Bomber Command from 1943 onwards was in part due to the use of air-to-air missiles by Luftwaffe nightfighters. The mind boggles at what results the Germans might have achieved if they had fitted similar guidance systems to their VI and V2 ground-to-ground missiles, which became operational in the summer of 1944. Meanwhile, the standard British rocket was an unguided projectile with a 60lb high explosive warhead.

British interest in guided missiles did not become active until 1947 when the long range test facility was opened at Woomera in the Australian desert. The main reason for this was the development of the British nuclear bomb and it was not until the following year that the British aviation industry took its first tentative steps into guided missile production when Fairey, De Havilland, Vickers, English Electric and Bristol all formed missile departments.

The development of these weapons was carried on in complete secrecy. Whole workforces were screened for security and quite willingly spent their working day assembling and testing missiles out of sight of their fellow employees. The project was known in the works as the Job 1220 and by 1951 a new research laboratory for missile work had arisen on Filton Hill.

Air Staff policy allocated development to each aircraft company – independent missile producers were kept strictly at bay – and so it was arranged that Fairey and De Havilland would build the first British air-to-air missiles and a contract to Bristols would cover a surface-to-air defence system. Code-named 'Red Duster' the missile would in due course become the production version of the famous Bristol Bloodhound Mk. I and II and would provide a large part of the defence of the U.K. for the better part of three decades.

The Bloodhound had an overall length of 25ft, which included a nuclear warhead in certain circumstances, a pair of 9ft $3^1/_2$ in. span stub wings and two Bristol Thor ram-jets. These latter were ignited only after the weapon had been boosted to Mach 1 in its own length by four R.A.F. Gosling solid rockets each of which developed 25,000 lb.s.t. The Thor ram-jets used ordinary Avtur aviation kerosene and took over from the rockets after the latter had used four seconds of flight. The weapon was controlled on the way to its selected target by radar equipment developed by Bristol's partners in the venture, the Ferranti Corporation of Edinburgh.

Development of Bloodhound was well underway by late 1949 and initial tests carried out at Aberporth, West Wales and at Woomera. The weapon proved to have a a theoretical radius of 40 miles, though in practice this was nearer 20 miles. It also proved to possess an impressive ceiling. The Mk. I could see off targets flying between 10,000 and 59,000 feet while the Mark II extended this between 150 and 60,000 feet.

The first Bristol-Ferranti Bloodhound Mk.I surface-to-air missiles were deployed with No. 264 Squadron at R.A.F. Station, North Coates, Lincolnshire in July 1958 and commissioned on 1 December of that year. Many repeat orders for Bloodhound would follow and the Guided Weapons Division at Filton would provide the foundations of research, development and manufacture that would provide its successors, the British Aircraft Corporation, with skills and facilities the equal of any in the world. The struggle for Britannia and the Proteus rescue under Hooker had saved Bristol, but only just. Now, just when a period of investment and re-organisation would have benefited the Filton and Patchway plants, they were to be thrown into the hands of a new management even as the aircraft side faced shutdown. The weapons business was a thriving concern with much future potential and must have provided encouragement to Sir Reginald Verdon-Smith as he opened talks with Bristol's future partners, H.G.Nelson (later Lord Nelson of Stafford) of English Electric and Sir Charles Dunphie, Managing Director of Vickers (Hunting Aircraft joined later) on 19 January 1960. For Bristol Aviation, a new age, with new ways and partners was about to dawn.

8

CONCORDE

1960 – 1976

'I start from the premise that air travel is in essence about speed, and that faster communication is to the benefit of mankind as a whole.'

Geoffrey Knight in *Concorde – the Inside Story* (1976).

When the Second World War ended in August 1945, it is a matter of historical record that there were commercially active in Great Britain 27 airframe design and construction companies and eight aircraft engine companies. Two of the aircraft plants were owned by Vickers and a further four in loose if independent membership of the Hawker Siddeley Group. These diverse concerns had grown up between the wars when sufficient resources in the shape of civil or military orders were forthcoming. Most of them were headed by outstanding personalities from the pioneering days who had gathered rising young men around them. At Hawker Siddeley, Sir Thomas Sopwith could boast Sir Roy Dobson, Sir Frank Spriggs and Sir Sidney Camm. Sir Frederick Handley Page pursued his authoritative way, the Fairey family ran Fairey and at Rolls, as we have seen, was the massive figure of Lord Hives. Bristol was no exception in that control of the Bristol Aeroplane Company Ltd, the holding company, remained firmly in control of the White and Verdon-Smith families, even if Peter Masefield, outgoing Chief Executive of British European Airways was appointed Managing Director of Bristol Aircraft Ltd on 1 January 1956. The arrangement did not endure for long.

This network of largely family companies now matched its commercial and work practices to a great leap forward in the technology of aviation, led by the emergence of the gas turbine as the primary source of power for flight. Research, particularly in metallurgy, became increasingly expensive while, at the same time, the Labour Government of 1945-51 took all major airlines into state ownership and so the Government became the industry's largest and almost only domestic customer! However, the outbreak of the Cold War and the Korean War of 1950 sparked a rearmament boom and by mid-1955 the British industry was employing 250,000 with most of the 27 airframe companies still in being.

To those who could read these signs, the writing was already on the wall. In 1953 the industry produced approximately 2000 aircraft. As 1957 approached, the figure was down to 968 (34%). By 1960 these figures were forecast to be 510. Now a decision was taken which proved to be right, albeit for the wrong reasons.

The 1957 Defence White Paper, produced by the Secretary of State Duncan Sandys, had a cataclysmic effect on the aircraft industry. In a nutshell, Sandys argued that all future wars would be nuclear in character and therefore all weapons in future would be automatically operated. The days of the manned aircraft in warfare were at an end. Sandys and his advisors were wrong but at a stroke the industry had lost its entire military order book with the exception of the English Electric supersonic fighter and the possible replacement for the Canberra bomber. The situation led to a meeting of the Government and the industry held in September 1957. Grouping followed rapidly, and although the formal foundation of the British Aircraft Corporation did not take place until 1 July 1960 the two intervening years saw much hard negotiation. This centred around the Canberra replacement contract, or Tactical Strike Reconnaissance (TSR) 2 which was awarded jointly to Vickers and English Electric, so that these companies each took 40% of the shares of B.A.C. while Bristol took the remaining 20% with its aircraft and weapon systems. This was only after exhaustive discussions had taken place with Hawkers who chose, literally at the eleventh hour, to join with De Havilland as part of the Hawker Siddeley concern. From here it was a natural step for Sir Reginald to meet with Lord Knollys, the Vickers Chairman of the time.

So it was that a new figure took the Filton stage in the ebullient form of Sir George Edwards, the formidable Chief Engineer of Vickers Aviation and now to become Managing Director of B.A.C. He was joined on the Board by Sir Reginald Verdon-Smith and William Masterton.

The TSR2 had already made its mark on Bristol in another connection. Government policy required that the two power plants for the new machine should be handled by another consortium, this time in the engine business. After some support from Vickers for the Rolls-Royce Medway, the choice fell on the Olympus 22R which Hooker was developing at Patchway but the two concerns of Bristol and Armstrong Siddeley had to unite in order to get the joint contract, the resulting company emerging in late 1959 as Bristol-Siddeley Engines Ltd. In 1961, De Havilland and Blackburn Engines were added to the stable. Sir Reginald Verdon-Smith became Chairman of the joint concern and when it was eventually taken over by Rolls-Royce in 1966, he became Vice-Chairman of that company. There is little doubt that Verdon-Smith would have avoided amalgamation of the Bristol Aeroplane Company's engine interests if at all possible. However, despite the great efforts of Hooker and Coryton, the struggle for survival during the Proteus crisis had debilitated the Company's resources and amalgamation was the only course if development of Hooker's designs was to proceed.

The origins of the great Bristol Olympus date back to 1946 when Frank Owner sought studies for a military turbo-jet for long-range bombers. The result was the first ever twin-spool turbo-jet, having two axial spools in series each driven by its own turbine. When Hooker arrived at Patchway in 1949, the design stage was well advanced and the engine was tested for the first time on 16 May 1950. Unlike the Proteus, the Olympus was a great engine from the start. The engine was under production for the great Avro Vulcan V bomber but two of the early versions were fitted for test purposes to an English Electric Canberra. This machine, piloted by Walter Gibb, Assistant Chief Test Pilot, set a new world height for Class C Aeroplanes on 29 August 1955 of 65,890ft (20,083 mtrs). The same aircraft WD592, also piloted by Gibb, had earlier established a previous best of 63,668ft on 3 May 1953.

In 1956 Hooker commenced a redesign of the Olympus, increasing the airflow through the engine to 240lb/sec. and upping the thrust to 17000lb. He failed to get Ministry backing for this but was supported by Sir Reginald who backed the engine commercially. Then the Ministry of Supply withdrew all support from the Olympus, opting for the Rolls-Royce Conway instead. There now developed a Company versus Ministry battle in which Verdon-Smith triumphed by the expedient of absorbing development costs on his own budget and thus under-pricing Rolls. So the exceptional commercial judgement and courage of this remarkable man again served his Company and country. So it was that, just as proposals for TSR2 and an SST transport were looking feasible at the end of the fifties, Bristol was able to offer exactly the engine that these types required. In addition, other versions of the Olympus were used to power Royal Navy warships, including the *Invincible* class aircraft carriers and many others were used in electrical power stations. As for the Conway, it powered the Victor tanker and some B.O.A.C. versions of Boeing jetliners but little else and soon went out of production.

Another engine from the fifties produced at Patchway that deserves mention here is the Orpheus, a lightweight turbo-jet which first ran on 17 December 1954 which Hooker created for W.E.W. Petter's small Folland Gnat fighter. The Orpheus was subsequently chosen by NATO to power all contestants in a light fighter contest won by the Fiat G91 and many thousands of the engine were built at Bristol and also under licence by KHD, Fiat and Hindustan Aeronautics. In 1956, Hooker's team began design studies for an engine employing vectored thrust for vertical take off. Based on schemes of the French designer Wilbault, the engines used the same power plant for both vertical and horizontal flight. As the engine was based on a military design, in 1958 it was not officially permitted to exist and so Sir Reginald once again backed an idea which Government spurned. At Hawker Sir Sydney Camm also went ahead with an airframe to suit the engine. All this would one day result in the Hawker Harrier, the brilliant VTOL fighter which did more than any other aircraft to win the Falklands War for Great Britain.

The early days of 1960 found the Filton factory facing a desperate situation. At the formation of B.A.C., Britannia production was almost complete and a new project badly needed if the workforce was to be retained. Work of a sort existed in ten sets of wings to be designed for the Short Belfast, a large transport for the R.A.F. This machine was being built in Northern Ireland for political reasons to boost the Ulster economy and Filton supplied the wings overland. The aircraft first flew on 5 January 1964 and all ten were completed at the end of 1966. Design studies were already underway on a large car-ferry transport and the first ideas for supersonic airliners but these were very far from producing anything approaching

Walter Gibb about to begin one of his world height record-breaking flights in Canberra WD592.
He did it twice – on 3 May 1955 (63,668ft) and on 29 August 1955 (65,890ft).

Two chief test pilots. A.J. (Bill) Pegg right who succeeded Uwins in 1947, congratulates Walter Gibb on
his world height record in 1953. Gibb eventually took over on Pegg's retirement from flying.

A vectored duct from the Bristol Pegasus STOL turbo-fan engine which first ran in 1959. Developed versions have flown with several airforces and naval air arms. This was the engine that made victory possible for Great Britain in the Falklands War of 1982.

The Short Belfast military transport for which Filton built the wings under sub-contract.

the cutting of metal. The only other machine currently being made at Filton was the Type 188; an all stainless steel experimental research machine, two of which were being assembled in conditions of utmost secrecy for the Ministry of Supply. Russell's team had explored several promising designs in the post-war years such as the Types 172, 174 and 176 but all available funds went to the Britannia programme. So Bristol's first pure jet waited as late as a 1953 specification ER.134, which called for an aircraft capable of sustained flight at twice the speed of sound to carry out kinetic heating research.

Six examples of the 188 were originally ordered, later reduced to a full-scale test specimen and two prototypes. The design called for an all stainless steel structure and this was bonded together by a technique developed in Filton's structural research laboratories known as puddle welding. This technique required close quality control as wrong heat settings could easily blow holes in the structure, and it was a triumph for the production team that eventually two aircraft were completed. These were led again by the formidable Frank Chard, with F.J. Burnell in charge of the assembly team. The design team was under the direction of Dr Russell with H.S. (Tug) Liner in day-to-day control.

The first prototype was rolled out on 26 April 1961 but continuous technical problems delayed the first flight until April 1962 when the Company's chief test pilot, Godfrey Auty, delivered the machine (XF923) in a 23 minute flight to Boscombe Down. The second Type 188 (XF926) followed into the air on 29 April 1963 in the hands of the same pilot but neither aeroplane saw much service, the fuel consumption of the two De Havilland Gyron Junior DGJ 10 turbo-jets proving so excessive that any worthwhile endurance for research flight proved unattainable. One of the 188s is today preserved in the Cosford R.A.F. Museum, near Wolverhampton.

The success of the Olympus and its use in Vulcan and TSR2 meant that, as amalgamation neared completion in 1961, the old Fedden factory at Patchway faced the future under Coryton and Hooker with contThe Bloodhound weapon system was in full production but on the aircraft side the tiny 188 was the only machine on the order book. Re-organisation had left the design studies for the British supersonic airliner (SST) under Russell's control but orders were a long way off and Filton badly needed work if the factory was to survive.

Sir George Edwards now transferred some VC10 work from Weybridge and more importantly, moved responsibilty for development of the big two-seat version of the Lightning fighter from Preston. This was sufficient to keep Filton in business until the B.A.C.111 contract came along, followed by the SST programme.

The decision to build the first Mark 5 Lightnings at Filton led to a constructive and cordial liaison with the ex-English Electric sites in the Preston area. Filton produced the Mark 5 from earlier Mark 4 aircraft and flew the first of two off on 29 March 1962 with Preston test pilot Jimmy Dell at the controls. Thereafter, a production line in the west bay of the Assembly Hall produced the front fuselage of a further batch of twenty, the first of which flew, piloted by Jimmy Dell, on 17 July 1964. Two accident replacements and a further seven for Saudi Arabia and Kuwait followed.

Work sharing based on available capacity became Board policy. Into the B.A.C. empire came Filton and Cardiff from Bristol, Weybidge and Hurn from Vickers, Preston, Warton, Salmesbury, Accrington and weapons plants at Luton and Stevenage from English Electric while the stable was completed by the Hunting Aircraft factory at Luton.

B.A.C. was to be welded into a cohesive aviation manufacturing company, competing on a worldwide basis. The weapons factories were fully occupied and three new major aircraft projects were underway. First was the TSR2 which from the start was to prove an exceptional aircraft in terms of anticipated performance and ease of production. TSR2 provided little work at Filton other than orders for minor components but it was of vital interest to Patchway which supplied its two Olympus power plants. Behind the reluctance to place more work at Filton was the possibility of production orders for the Bristol 208 Freighter (which never came to fruition) and schemes for the Bristol 223 supersonic transport which eventually emerged as the Anglo-French Concorde, the second of B.A.C.'s new projects which would preoccupy Filton for the next decade and a half.

Finally, there was the B.A.C.111, a medium-size regional jet-liner which derived from the Hunting H. 107 which B.A.C. inherited at the take over. Sir George Edwards was convinced that there was a market

The Bristol Type 188 Stainless Steel Research Aircraft (35ft 1in span, 2 x 14000pst DH Gyron Junior DGJ, 1400 mph plus) is rolled out on 26 April 1961. The production manager, Fred Burnell is at the centre of the picture. This aircraft XF923, the first of two, flew on 14 April 1962 but the project was of limited value due to duration problems.

The first Type 188 streaming its braking parachute at Filton, just before first flight on 14 April 1962.

The Type 188 in flight.

*Godfrey Auty, the Bristol Aircraft Chief Test Pilot,
who took both Types 188 on their maiden flights
from Filton to A. and A.E., Boscombe Down.*

Filton personalities. Sir Reginald Verdon-Smith (1912-1992), Chairman of B.A.C., left, makes a presentation to Sir George White (1913-1983) the third baronet. Sir Reginald led the Company during the Britannia crisis and went on to be a dominant and respected figure in the aircraft industry. Sir George pioneered the Bristol car business which became a by-word for automotive quality.

for a short-range twin jet in the U.S.A. He persuaded his Board that a bold decision would get in ahead of Douglas and Boeing. So in May 1961, B.A.C. decided to go ahead with a production line and an initial order for twenty aircraft of the B.A.C.111 type, later to be called One-Eleven. The move provided both good and bad news for Bristol.

The bad news was that an earlier plan to use Bristol-Siddeley BS75 engines in the new aircraft was changed in favour of the Rolls-Royce RB163 which would become the Spey. This was a considerable blow to Patchway and dismayed Sir Reginald Verdon-Smith. He predicted a fierce reaction from American manufacturers and was proved correct as the Douglas DC9 and Boeing 737 owe their origin at least in part to early sales in the U.S.A. of the B.A.C.111. The good news was that the component manufacture of the One-Eleven would be shared by B.A.C. factories. Filton got the whole rear fuselage and tail sub-assembly and a production line was established in No.2 Flight Shed which had earlier seen the assembly of the

Brabazon fuselage and the two Type 188s. Production was in the charge of George Gedge, who had started his career with Shorts at Rochester on flying boats, then spent much of the war supporting the Stirling bomber in service and gone on to run the Short's Britannia line at Queens Island, Belfast. His success on B.A.C.111 rear ends would eventually lead to the managing directorship of Filton and control of all Concorde production.

The B.A.C.111 proved, by British standards, to be an unqualified success, even after a major set-back at the beginning of its career. The prototype flew for the first time from Hurn on 26 August 1963 with Jock Bryce at the controls but two months later, on 22 October, this aircraft was lost during flight tests due to an uncontrollable stall developing with CofG in the full aft condition. The highly skilled test crew of seven, including pilot Mike Lithgow all died in the crash. Suitably modified after this tragic setback, the B.A.C.111 prospered and was in production from 1961 until B.A.C. was nationalised in 1977 and beyond. By the autumn of 1980, sales had reached 230.

The success of the One-Eleven was to prove critical to B.A.C., when in 1965 it suffered a major set-back. Development of the TSR2 had gone smoothly and the prototype made its maiden flight from the experimental airfield at Boscombe Down, Wiltshire on 27 September, 1964. It was piloted by Roland 'Bee' Beamont with Don Bowen as navigator. Beamont was later to say of the TSR2 that 'we had in our grasp one of the most remarkable designs in aviation industry'. The following month a Labour Government, led by Harold Wilson, was elected with a majority of four and subsequent events led to the conclusion that Labour had already decided to cancel TSR2 while still in opposition.

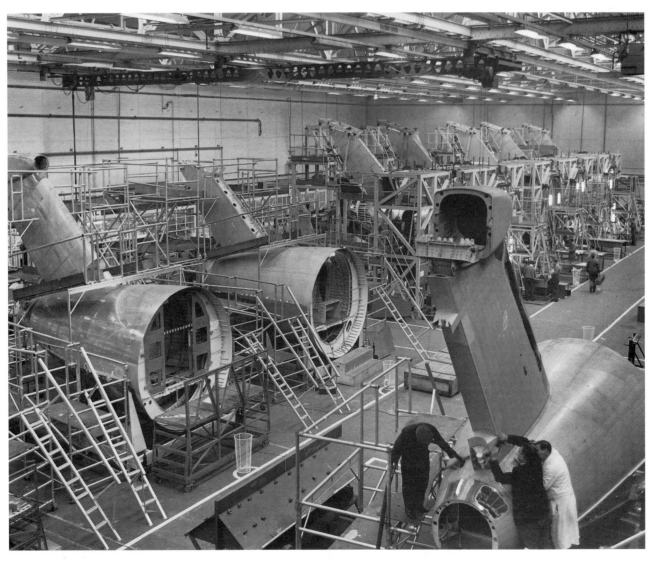

Sternframes for the BAC 111 production line under assembly at Filton in the late sixties. Over 200 aircraft sets were supplied to BAC Hurn, and later a limited order to Romania which built the aircraft under licence.

The country's economic weakness would lead to various cancellations of aviation projects but that of TSR2 was the most tragic and important in its consequences. The outgoing Conservative Government had already reduced defence expenditure which resulted in B.A.C. losing the contract for Blue Water, a large nuclear warhead ground-to-ground weapon.

The early years of B.A.C. guided weapon affairs had not been happy due to the rivalries of Filton and Stevenage and in March 1963, inspired by the Blue Water affair, moves were made to weld the weapons business into more workable shape. The Guided Weapons Division was formed with Sir George as Chairman, Lord Caldecote Managing Director, the rapidly rising George Jefferson Chief Executive and David Farrar Technical Director. Also on this Board was James Harper, General Manager of Bristol Aircraft and currently leading Filton. A man of great promise, he would have achieved great things if he had not been struck down by a crippling illness which led to his premature death.

Jack Jefferies, who had opened the Cardiff factory, was now Guided Weapons Production Manager. He would eventually succeed George Gedge as Chief Executive for the whole Filton site. In April 1964 Jefferson transferred to Filton half the total contract for development of the Rapier anti-aircraft missile, including the launcher and fire units. Rapier became a major Filton project that was to last two decades and beyond.

These changes were all made with the one objective of conserving resources overall for the TSR2 but to no avail. On 15 January 1965, Harold Wilson invited the leaders of the aircraft industry to dinner at Chequers. Sir George Edwards and Sir Reginald Verdon-Smith were present. No commitment on the future of the TSR2 was given, and this led to a Cabinet decision on 31 March 1965 to completely abandon the project. This was announced in Chancellor Callaghan's budget speech on 6 April, a particularly insensitive method of disclosure in that management had no opportunity to warn the workforce of the decision. The gaping void in the R.A.F.'s equipment was to be replaced by the American machines Phantom and F111A. In practice, the F111 proved unable to perform its expected role and British orders were later cancelled. Later it was alleged that the British Ministry of Defence knew that the F111 was in trouble before TSR2 was cancelled.

The demise of TSR2 seared the British aircraft industry as few incidents before or since. Not only was an outstanding aircraft lost but 8000 redundancies (5000 at B.A.C.) ensued and the factory at Luton closed, the second major closure in the town in three years. Production of the Jet Provost, the R.A.F. basic trainer was transferred to Preston. Only the substantial order book for the One-Eleven, which by this time was in full production, allowed B.A.C. to survive. Fortunately, Olympus development was underway at Patchway for the SST and the impact of the loss of FSR2 was not as traumatic as it could have been. In his memoirs, Hooker is dismissive of the merits of multi-role aircraft but there is no doubt that the Bristol engine plant owes much to the existence of SST.

The proposal to build an airliner travelling at supersonic speed dates from 1954 and, curiously, originated in a government agency, rather than as a proposal from the commercial aircraft industry. The Royal Aircraft Establishment at Farnborough was considering some studies, the purpose of which was to regain the lost momentum of British aviation following the Comet disasters which had allowed the American industry to capture the world long-haul market with its first generation pure-jets, the Boeing 707 and the Douglas DC8. The British state-owned airline formed a relationship with Boeing which has persisted to this day, often to the detriment of the domestic industry – the Vickers VC7, for example, being discarded in favour of the American Boeing 707.

Farnborough reached the conclusion that the next logical step was for Britain to go for a SST aircraft and so advised the Government, which for once acted with commendable speed. It set up the Supersonic Transport Aircraft Committee (STAC) under the chairmanship of the R.A.E. Deputy Director, M.B. (later Sir Morien) Morgan. On STAC were represented all the major airframe and engine manufacturers and Archibald Russell and Stanley Hooker were there from Bristol. The influence of both men on the final committee report was crucial and they would go on to be the major design leaders of the aircraft that would eventually be Concorde.

STAC faced many problems in producing a practical proposal, the two major ones being the sonic boom and kinetic heating. In the first case, as an aircraft approaches the speed of sound, it creates in effect a bow wave which meets the air ahead with a boom which can be dangerous to listeners and physically destructive to ground structures in certain extreme cases. The other problem, kinetic heating, arises from the temperature of an aircraft skin increasing as the square of the speed (in m.p.h.). At twice the speed of sound the temperature of the aircraft rises 182 degrees. Even allowing for the SST operating in temperatures down to -50 degrees C, a rise of 130 degrees has to be dealt with.

STAC began work on 5 November 1956. Ahead lay three years of patient study and research, among which was brilliant work on delta wings by Dietrich Kuchemann who worked at R.A.E. from 1946 until his death in 1976. Both Russell and Hooker were in close touch with the committee as its work developed and it eventually reported on 9 March 1959, recommending that two designs be developed – a 100-seat aircraft with a speed of Mach 1.2 and 1500 mile range and a 150 seater with a trans-atlantic capability. From the Bristol point of view, the latter proposal made far more sense. The experience of the Type 188 had already convinced Dr Russell that a stainless steel/titanium design with Mach 3 capability was not practical in terms of cost and programme. Later, the American industry would spend $20 billion before abandoning the scheme. 'Russ' had by now been joined in the SST team by two other personalities who would play large parts in the Concorde story, his Chief Engineer, Dr W.J. 'Bill' Strang and Chief Aerodynamicist M.G. 'Mick' Wilde. Together this team developed the first Bristol SST design, the Type 198, powered by six of Hooker's Olympus and at 380,000 lb take-off weight considered to be too heavy. The design was later developed into the Type 223 at 250,000 lb, 100 seats and a trans-atlantic range.

Dr W.J. (Bill) Strang, Filton's senior engineer who took over Concorde
design on the retirement of Sir Archibald Russell.

*M.G. (Mick) Wilde, who took the lead in engineering Concorde air intakes,
the critical factor in the creation of a supersonic aircraft. Wilde later
became Managing Director of the Filton factories.*

Until now the SST had been an all-British scheme but when a development contract was awarded to what was now B.A.C. in 1960, a condition was imposed by the British Government that the new corporation should seek an international partner to share the costs and the risks. There was no interest in the U.S.A. in such a project – Mach 3 was considered the target speed in Washington – and it must be said that throughout the SST programme Americans maintained a consistent opposition to the project.

An international partner was found in the giant French nationalised firm Sud-Aviation with headquarters at Saint Martin, near Toulouse. Sud had a design under development uncannily like that of 'Russ' and his team which the French called the Super-Caravelle, a model of which they produced at the 1961 Paris Air Show. Discussions began at both government and company level. Eventually, on 29 November 1962 an Anglo-French treaty to jointly produce an SST was signed in London by Julian Amery, Minister of Supply and the French Ambassador, M. de Courcel. This was despite last minute efforts by the U.S. Government to persuade the British to pull out.

The agreement provided for Britain to take the lead on engine production through Bristol-Siddeley and the Olympus with the French engine firm SNECMA doing the nozzle. France would get 60% of airframe manufacture but even so B.A.C. got forward and rear fuselage, droop nose, fin, rudder and the entire engine nacelles, including intakes and engine bay doors. There was to be no duplication of

Sir George Edwards (b. 1908) is shown third from the left in this photo from the early days of Concorde. Sir George was instrumental in gaining vital work for the Bristol factory at a low ebb in its fortunes. On his left is M. Andre Turcat, who was Chief Test Pilot of Aerospatiale and first took Concorde into the air. Turcat later became a Member of the European Parliament.

City of Bristol

An Olympus Series 593 gas turbine, the great engine that Stanley Hooker developed for the Concorde supersonic airliner.

manufacture until assembly when two production lines would operate, one at Toulouse and the other at Filton. Thus the outlines of the project were drawn and in the agreement included a mandatory 'no break' clause. Years later, Julian Amery told the author that this clause was at his insistence because he feared French withdrawal at some time in the future. In the event, this clause prevented Labour Governments on two occasions, in 1964 and 1974, from withdrawing unilaterally from the project.

As part of the development programme, Filton was modifying the first Fairey F.D.2 WG774 to a design which included a complete new wing in ogee form to obtain data for Concorde. The F.D. 2 had once held the world airspeed record but by the time it arrived at Filton it was already an ageing aircraft. The well tried team of Frank Chard and Fred Burnell was assigned the task of up-dating this curious little aeroplane and there was much exasperation, particularly over the many weeks spent in trying to regain cabin pressurisation with the many loose rivets in the old fuselage. Eventually the difficulties were overcome and the aircraft made its second 'maiden' flight from Filton in the hands of Godfrey Auty on 1 May 1964. Because of the radical redesign, 'Russ' had given it a Bristol type number and as the Bristol 221 it was the last Bristol type number to fly. Today, the Type 221 is preserved at the Fleet Air Arm Museum, Yeovilton.

Work now went ahead on both sides of the English Channel and commuting between Filton and Toulouse became a commonplace experience for Bristol employees. From the first, there were management clashes both on design and production problems and the fact that neither side had any control over the other led to poor management control. Even so personal relationships were usually excellent and many were to survive the Concorde days into the brilliant series of Airbus designs. In 1963, both B.O.A.C. and Air France signed Concorde sales options, and were soon joined by Pan American. By May 1967 these 'options' would stand at 74 from 16 airlines.

Assembly of the first British Concorde commenced at Filton in August 1966, four months behind the French machine. This aircraft was rolled out on 11 December 1967 and made its first flight on 2 March 1969, with Andre Turcat as pilot. Brian Trubshaw took the British prototype 002 into the air from Filton a month later on 9 April. The prototypes then engaged in an intensive round of development flying.

The last aircraft to fly with a Bristol type number, the Type 221(25ft span, 14000pst R.R.Avon RA28R, 1060 mph) was converted at Filton from a Fairey FD2 and fitted with new ogee-form wings for research flying on the SST project which became Concorde. This aircraft is preserved at the Fleet Air Arm Museum, Yeovilton.

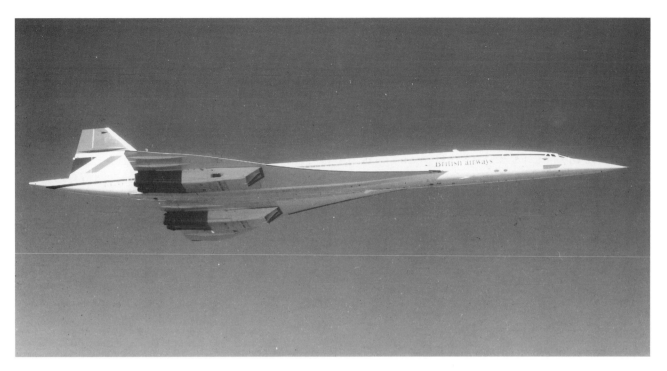

The second Concorde to be supplied to British Airways, No. 206, G-BOAA.

A Concorde taking off in bad weather conditions amid spectacular spray patterns over the wings.

The British Concorde assembly line in the centre bay of the Assembly Hall at Filton.

A Concorde in the aircraft 'dock' at Filton.

The rather ungainly approach of a Concorde landing.

The story of Concorde is well known. Two aspects however must be discussed as these led to the ultimate production numbers of the aircraft being limited to six for British Airways and seven for Air France. The first was the environmental impact, particularly the sonic boom. Fears of the effect of this had already led the Government to insist that Concorde flight testing would be done at the R.A.F. base at Fairford in Gloucestershire, away from the Bristol built-up area where Tony Wedgwood Benn, the Minister currently responsible for the project, had his constituency. The French machines continued to use St Martin which was as close to central Toulouse as Filton to Bristol. As soon as test flying at high Mach numbers began over the Irish Sea, claims for damage to glasshouses poured in from Cornish market gardeners and an anti-Concorde culture sprang into life. This was actively encouraged by the U.S., especially after Congress dropped the American SST on 24 March 1971. Soon, New York had imposed a Concorde ban and Middle and Far Eastern governments were refusing to allow the aircraft to fly over their territory. All these problems and objections did much to delay the aircraft's entry into airline service but one by one they were eventually overcome. Even so, there was a time when the only place that it was possible to fly a Concorde from London was to Bahrain on the Persian Gulf. Everywhere else was prohibited for political reasons.

The second aspect, and by far the most critical, was cost. When the Anglo-French treaty was signed in November 1962, the estimated joint cost was £150 - £170 million. In the fifteen years or so that Concorde took from first to last, the actual costs worked out at £40 million per year of which half was found by the British taxpayer. About 50% of the increase went in inflation costs but this still left over £400 million increase on the original estimate. The immediate consequence was that in January 1973, both Pan AM and TWA announced that they would not be buying Concorde after all and they were followed in due course by all other prospective purchasers except B.A. and Air France.

A jubilant Tony Benn, Aviation Minister and Bristol M.P. (left) with Chief Test Pilot Brian Trubshaw
after a flight in Concorde prototype 102. Benn was a resolute supporter of the project.

Despite all this, the Concorde programme remains one of the great technical triumphs of the twentieth century. To have placed it in service subject to all the safety requirements of a subsonic airliner and obtain full airworthiness certification is on the same level of achievement as the Apollo programme which eventually placed a handful of Americans on the moon. Until the tragic event of August 2000 Concorde had carried thousands of passengers millions of miles in complete safety at supersonic speeds for most of their journeys.

By the time Concorde entered airline service in January 1976, the bill to nationalise the aircraft industry was already before the House of Commons. By then the Bristol aero-engine factory at Patchway had passed into state ownership in most unfortunate circumstances. In October 1966, Bristol-Siddeley Engines was bought out by Rolls-Royce for £63.6 million and so control of Patchway passed to Rolls-Royce at Derby. Ostensibly the reason for the bid was to prevent B.S.E.L. linking up with the American giant Pratt and Whitney to produce the new generation of higher by-pass ratio engines. Incredibly, the Rolls Chairman Sir Denning Pearson had no place for Stanley Hooker on his Board, although Sir Reginald Verdon-Smith became Vice-Chairman. Hooker therefore retired on 30 September 1967, his sixtieth birthday.

Two years later Verdon-Smith found himself embroiled in a distateful affair which was not of his making. Early in 1968, it emerged that between 1959 and 1963, B.S.E.L. had made excessive profits in the so-called 'double charging' affair. The irony was that if Sir Reginald had not immediately informed the Government when the matter came to light, no one would have been any the wiser. Although he had been Chairman of B.S.E.L. at the time, it was accepted by the Public Accounts Committee that

Verdon-Smith was not to blame. Not so the Minister, Bristol M.P. Tony Wedgwood Benn who insisted on his resignation from all public appointments. A man of great principle, Sir Reginald found this distressing and resigned from Rolls-Royce. Also he did not take up the chairmanship of Lloyds Bank, where he had been Chairman-elect since 1967.

Industry in general now rallied to Sir Reginald's side. The leaders of 14 major firms along with the President and Director of the C.B.I. wrote to *The Times* deploring the incident and the slight on Verdon Smith's integrity. The following year he received a huge vote of confidence when he was elected to succeed Lord Portal as Chairman of British Aircraft Corporation, a post he held with distinction until his retirement in 1972. From 1973 to 1979 he was Chairman of Lloyds Bank International and also continued his service as Pro-Chancellor of Bristol University. He died on 21 June 1992.

When Rolls-Royce bought out B.S.E.L. in 1966, they effectively became owners of the Bristol Aeroplane Company which now in reality ceased to exist as its 20% interest in B.A.C. passed to Rolls. After a period of much uncertainty when Rolls, egged on by the Labour Government, planned the sale of the Bristol shares to B.A.C.'s arch-rival Hawker-Siddeley, the situation was saved by Sir Arnold Weinstock, Chairman of G.E.C. (owners of English Electric) who backed B.A.C.'s purchase of the shares from Rolls.

Even after the merger, affairs at Patchway and Derby went along on much the same separate paths. Patchway was busy on Olympus for Concorde and other applications. Then there was Pegasus and the new engine for the European multi-role Combat Aircraft (M.R.C.A.). Matters at Derby were less

The Panavia Tornado Multi-role Combat Aircraft, jointly built by the UK, Germany and Italy, first flew in August 1974 and was powered by two Turbo-union RB199 3-spool turbo-fan engines, in which the Bristol plant played a leading part, producing several hundred.

A group of Filton management in the late seventies. The Works Director, Jack Jefferies, is in the centre with Fred Burnell on his left.

satisfactory. There development and production was proceeding on the RB211, the engine selected by Lockheed for its new wide-bodied jet, the L1011 Tristar. Bereft of Verdon-Smith's judgement and in many technical difficulties, by 1970 Rolls were in deep trouble on the SB211 but were unable to get any relief from Lockheed who rightly stuck to the terms of their contract. Stanley Hooker was tempted out of retirement to advise on the technical problems but was not in time to prevent Rolls being put into liquidation in February 1971.

The new Conservative Government under Edward Heath had little option but to set up a new state-owned company, Rolls-Royce (1971) Ltd, and although they specifically refused to buy the RB211, they paid its daily costs until funds started flowing from Lockheed, who signed up a new contract on 11 May 1971. So, twenty-two years after he parted company with Lord Hives, Hooker became Technical Director of Rolls-Royce and set about the task of rescuing the RB211. This he did successfully and finally retired in 1978.

The idea of nationalisation went back as far as 1964, when the Wilson Government appointed the Plowden committee to report on the future of Britain's aircraft industry. Although the report was shelved, it left a firm conviction within the Labour Party and the Trade Unions that the best course was to take aviation into state ownership and the Labour Government elected in October 1974 had such a commitment in its manifesto. Nearly three years were needed to get a bill through Parliament.

These years saw the retirement of some of the industry's major figures. Dr Russell had retired with a well-earned knighthood in 1970 and in 1975 Sir George Edwards laid down his many responsibilities. He was succeeded as Chairman of B.A.C. by Allen Greenwood. The nationalisation legislation became effective on 29 April 1977 and the Bristol aircraft factories passed into the control of British Aerospace Corporation, a state-owned company with a politician (Lord Beswick) as Chairman. Seventy-six years and two months after Sir George White's visionary creation of Bristol aviation, the destiny of its descendants had passed from independent control.

9

IN THE NATIONAL INTEREST?

'Tell them there will be no more subsidies.'

Margaret Thatcher on the future of the aircraft industry in
conversation with the author – Bristol, April 1979.

When the ownership of the Filton factory and airfield passed to the state on 29 April 1977, it can be argued that the saga of the Bristol aeroplane ended. The engine plant at Patchway was already in the public sector and Rolls-Royce made its decisions at Derby and London, especially after Stanley Hooker retired for the second time in 1978, taking with him a well earned knighthood.

With nationalisation, the control of policy making and decision processes all passed to politicians and civil servants in London. There was no Bristol-based director on the organising committee that set up the structures of British Aerospace and no Bristol personality was nominated to the main board that took over on vesting day. Filton found itself a unit of the Aircraft Division of B.Ae and it would not be until the 1980s that Robert McKinley emerged to lead the B.Ae component of the European Airbus organisation which he did with great skill and success.

To the Filton work force, state ownership arrived unheralded and almost unnoticed. The factory was pre-occupied with the Concorde production programme and, while the political debate was at its height, British Airways and Air France commenced commercial services with the aircraft on 21 January 1976. Political and environmental restrictions still combined to keep Concorde off the North Atlantic and the first B.A. service was to Bahrain from London Heathrow while Air France operated from Paris to Rio de Janeiro. This same year saw the first flight of two Filton Concordes, 208 on 18 May and 210 on 25 August, while the gallant old prototype 202 was given a free transfer to the Science Museum and placed on permanent display at the Fleet Air Arm Museum at Yeovilton in Somerset. The other Concorde built for development, the pre-production 01, was retired to the Duxford branch of the Imperial War Museum in August 1977.

Services to New York began at last on 22 November 1977. Operated both from Paris and London, they have continued with reliability and until August 2000 little incident. Since the development debts were written off by the incoming Conservative Government as a precursor to the privatisation of the state airline British Airways, the machines have also operated profitably.

In many ways Concorde remained Filton's greatest triumph. The basic airframe and engine designs were British, schemed at Bristol by teams headed by Russell and Hooker. The author had a convincing demonstration of the capabilities of the machine in the summer of 1975 when he was asked to escort a group of Bristol V.I.P.s on one of the proving flights between London Heathrow and Gander in Newfoundland. The party assembled at Filton at noon on a Saturday and, after lunch, travelled by limousine to Heathrow along the M4. Then a Concorde, piloted by Brian Trubshaw, carried them across the Atlantic to Gander and back. The whole party was back in Bristol by 2200 hours!

Filton flew its last production Concorde (216) on 20 April 1979 and it was delivered to British Airways on 13 June of the following year. Registered as G-BOAF, this machine was the last complete aircraft to be assembled at Filton to date, and the chances of future complete assembly lines on the site are remote. The future of the factory would now lie in the production of components for national projects like the B.Ae 146 or multi-national efforts such as Airbus. Base servicing and modification programmes for the R.A.F. and the U.S.A.F. would be another source of profit and eventually plans would emerge to convert the site into a second civil airport for the Bristol region. But all this lay in the future as the new state-owned British Aerospace Corporation commenced what proved to be a short working life in April 1977. Filton joined with Weybridge to become a unit of the Aircraft Group with Michael G. Wilde as Managing Director.

A month after vesting day, in May 1977 there occurred an event that gave a clear indication of how the future appeared for Filton. Alan Greenwood, B.Ae's Deputy Chairman signed a protocol with the Romanian Trade Minister which set up contracts for the licencsed production of the B.A.C. 111 air-liner in Romania. The agreement was signed at Filton in June 1978 during a visit by the Romanian President Ceausescu and his wife who were on a state visit to this country.

The contract called for the supply of three complete aircraft to Bucharest and components for 22 more. This entailed opening up the rear fuselage assembly line at Filton and this was done in the old Experimental Department at the top of the hill. Restarting production is never easy. So it was with the re-juvenated One-Eleven. Nevertheless, production soon got back to normal and by the time Filton supplied its last rear fuselage to the assembly line at Hurn in March 1981, 237 copies had been supplied. The production run had occupied twenty years. The three aircraft for Romania were supplied in 1981/2. The first Romanian-assembled machine flew on 18 September 1982 and the complete transfer of production was complete by mid-1986.

In this same year of 1978, Filton obtained a contract that would lead to valuable and important business throughout the 1980s. The Yom Kippur War in October 1973 had a direct impact on world oil prices as the Arab states collaborated on a policy of high prices as an international political weapon. This led to high oil consumption countries, in particular the U.S.A., introducing energy-conservation policies. As a direct result, the U.S. Air Force adopted a policy of making modifications to their overseas based airfleets on site, rather than undertake the expense and fuel consumption of return to the United States. In addition, 1975 saw a relaxation of America's foreign trade regulations which led to an agreement between the two governments to service U.S. machines in the U.K.

The General Dynamics F-111 was a multi-role swing-wing military aircraft which was developed and produced for the U.S.A.F. and first flew on 21 December 1964. It was a contemporary of the TSR2 and was supposed to replace that machine's role in the R.A.F., following the latters cancellation. However the F-111 did not live up to design specifications, particularly at altitude and no orders were placed by the Ministry of Defence. Australia became the only overseas customer and the R.A.F. had to wait for the brilliant Panavia Tornado (M.R.C.A.) for its first variable geometry multi-role aircraft.

The F-111 entered service in October 1966 and soon proved to be a superb ground attack aircraft, particularly in the anti-tank role. By 1978, the U.S.A.F. had two wings of the aircraft based in Britain at Lakenheath in Suffolk and Upper Heyford in Oxfordshire. The first batch of work was confined to modification of the pyrotechnic section of the escape system while both sides tested each other's capabilities. In the event, the Filton workforce proved more than capable of dealing with the aircraft and contracts were soon in place which covered more than 40 depot maintenance tasks. This led to the construction of a cold proof test station and a paint shop which added two useful buildings to the complex.

A second five-year contract was signed in October 1988 covering 150 F-111s. By this time over 800 people were employed on the project which would last until the early nineties when the end of the Cold War led to defence expenditure reductions worldwide.

Another major project developed by B.Ae with government support was the B.Ae 146, a regional jetliner of very quiet performance. Its origins go back to 1973 when its design was commenced by Hawker Siddeley but no funding was available until after nationalisation when in July 1978 the Government gave the go-ahead. The final assembly of the machines was done at Hatfield but sub-assembly was spread around various B.Ae plants, more from a desire to spread work for political reasons than for productive efficiency. Bristol got the centre fuselage which carried the high mounted spar box and wing roots.

A ceremony held at Filton on 30 March 1984 to celebrate the delivery of the 100th F 111 to be 'relifed' for the USAF. A total of 270 had been delivered when the scheme ended in 1989.

A centre fuselage section for the BAe 146 feederliner which was built at Filton in the Assembly Hall and then delivered by road to Hatfield (and later Woodford) for assembly.

The 146 Series 100 made its first flight on 3 September 1981 and entered service with Dan Air as lead operator on 27 May 1983. Since then the machine has sold in a number of versions to operators in the U.S. and China, been chosen for Her Majesty's Royal Flight and in March 1990 a 146 became the first airliner to operate scheduled services into Antarctica. Although not enjoying huge commercial success, a second assembly line had been opened at Woodford near Manchester to cope, it was said, with increased orders. This was the reason given at the time, but the subsequent announcement in 1993 that Hatfield was to close caused raised eyebrows in some circles. At about the same time B.Ae announced that it was in negotiation with Taiwanese interests to assemble a version of the 146 in that island. The talks proved difficult and no decision had been reached by December 1993. By this time, the whole of B.Ae's business and small jetliner company was on the market.

A Series 300 BAe 146 in flight. The type first flew in September 1981 and enjoyed limited but steady production orders.

Other useful work in small quantities undertaken at Filton in the late seventies for B.Ae was machining of flap and slat rails and taileron skins for the Tornado MRCA, machined components for the Fokker-built version of the American F 16 Fighting Falcon and also nacelle and pylon components for RB211 engines fitted to Boeing 747s for British Airways. All this diverse work contributed to the steady profits announced annually by B.Ae.

This was just as well, because on 1 January 1981 British Aerospace returned to the private sector. The Conservative Government led by Margaret Thatcher that came to power in 1979 immediately commenced a radical programme of privatisation. The aerospace industry and British Airways were among the first batch of legislation, although somewhat cautiously the Government retained a 50% interest and it was not until 1985 that full privatisation was effected. The chairman of Esso Petroleum, Sir Austin Pearce, took over as Chairman of B.Ae and served with success until succeeded in 1987 by Professor Roland Smith.

Another interesting Filton project was the conversion of old Vickers VC 10 airliners into the B.A.C. VC 10 (K2 and K3) flying tankers. The importance of flight refuelling, first argued by Sir Alan Cobham in the thirties, was now becoming critical to the operational efficiencies of the R.A.F. and the VC 10 was chosen to replace the ageing Victors. During 1978, four ex-East African Airways and five ex-Gulf Air VC 10s arrived at Filton for eventual conversion. Primarily intended to refuel Tornado and Phantom fighters, the VC 10 tanker has two underwing hose drum units and one in the rear fuselage. Fuel tanks occupy much of the fuselage space. Conversion of these elderly machines proved a nightmare but eventually the first aircraft ZA 141 flew from Filton on 22 June 1982. Sufficient aircraft were ready for No. 101 Squadron at Brize Norton to begin operations in May 1984. A further order using old R.A.F. VC10s followed.

A clear example of the changed role of the Filton factory is this VC10 flying tanker. Between 1978 and 1985, nine VC10s were converted to the tanker role for the R.A.F. This is the first aircraft to be delivered–ZA 141.

The aviation success story of the 1980s was the emergence of the international partnership Airbus Industries which became a major player in the world airliner market and a viable challenger to Boeing's long held supremacy. British involvement in Airbus dates back to the mid-sixties when design studies by European manufacturers involved Hawker Siddeley. The principal players were Sud-Aviation of France and Deutsche Airbus of Germany but Hawker Siddeley was excluded due to the refusal of the then British Government to provide launching finance. Airbus Industrie was formed in December 1970 and work commenced on the wide-bodied A300 which made its maiden flight on 28 October 1972. The A300 entered service with Air France on the Paris-London route on 23 May 1974 by which time the original partners had been joined by Fokker and CASA, the Spanish airframe firm. Airbus success continued and the big breakthrough came in 1977 when the large American carrier Eastern Airlines placed orders for 29 aircraft. Although Airbus A300 was not sold to any other American airline, orders from elsewhere poured in. By 1978, Airbus had 23% of the market and was looking for further development.

This was provided by the A310, a slightly smaller version of the A300 with longer range and seating 218 passengers. B.Ae were already participating in a sub-contract role in designing and building wings and on 1 January 1979 it at last became a full partner in Airbus. B.Ae took 20% of the shares with Aerospatiale 37.9%, Deutsche Airbus 37.9% and CASA 4.2%.

The Airbus A310 prototype at Farnborough on a demonstration flight. This was the first Airbus design in which Filton was involved and the factory supplied the wing trailing edges, assembled in No. 3 Flight Shed.

A320 wings, having been equipped at Filton, are airlifted by Super-Guppy to Toulouse for final assembly.

Partnership in Airbus Industrie led to substantial new investment at Filton.
This is the new facility built for fitting out of Airbus A320 wings.

Wings components for Airbus A320 in production at Filton.

The Chester factory of B.Ae was selected to undertake the assembly of the wing box but Filton was allocated a large share of the trailing edges which were then transferred to Chester for assembly. A production line was set up in No. 3 Flight Shed and Filton's contribution to the Airbus story began. The first A310 flew on 3 April 1982, and the type entered service with Lufthansa and Swissair in March 1983. By 1990, orders for 229 A310s had been received.

Airbus went on to develop the A320, A330 and A340. As the nineties began it could offer a family of aircraft which could offer the short/medium haul 150-seat A320 and 186-seat A321, the medium/long range 218-seat A310 and 267-seat A300-600, the medium/long range 335-seat A330 and the very long range 295-seat A340. The latter two machines have interchangeable wings and control services with the obvious benefits for production that this brings. The first A340 entered service in 1994.

B.Ae manages its Airbus activity from its Airbus Division Headquarters at Filton. The prime responsibility is the design and manufacture of all Airbus wings as well as design and supply of the fuel system. For some Airbus models B.Ae also supplies the landing gear.

Filton's main task on the manufacturing side has been the equipping and completion of wings for the A320, on receipt of the wing box from Chester. The A320 programme was launched in March 1984 after the British Government had provided a repayable loan of £250 million for launching costs. The scheme included the construction of a $7 million new facility alongside the Assembly Hall at Filton which was opened by H.R.H. Princess Anne in September 1986.

The A320 first flew on 22 February 1987 and became familiar to the general public as the 'fly-by-wire' airliner because of its advanced flying controls which give pilots greater control within set limits, also providing weight saving and reduced servicing costs. The A320 was an instant success and in May 1987 the Government announced a further loan of £450 million to fund the starting costs of the A330/340. There was some speculation that this arrangement had something to do with the Department of Trade wishing to sell B.Ae the ailing state-owned Austin Leyland car manufacturers. By mid-1991, firm orders, from over 100 customers stood at 702 for the A300 and A310, 799 for the A320 and A321 and 247 for the A330/340. This totalled 1748 aircraft and options were already in place to take the total beyond 2000.

All this work however did not entirely protect the Filton plant from the impact of the depression. In addition B.Ae under Smith's chairmanship had acquired property interests which impacted on the future role of the group. In 1993 it became clear that Filton's future in aviation lay in its conversion into a civil airport and service base, a controversial proposal which led to immediate environmentalist protest. The future looked less than certain.

The years that followed the Rolls-Royce bankruptcy were not easy ones for the engine factory at Patchway but Stanley Hooker's redesign and rescue of the RB211 led to it being rated as one of the best of all the big-fan engines. But a long period of development lay ahead after its eventual entry into service in the Lockheed Tri-star. This version, the RB211-22B, was certificated in February 1973 and remained in production at Derby until 1982. Boeing has a long established policy of offering Rolls engines if the customer wished and later versions of the RB211 were fitted to the Boeing 747, 747-400 and 767. The RB535 version was fitted to 80% of Boeing 757s, while it was the first western engine to be fitted to a Russian airliner, the Tupolev Tu 205. The later version, the 524L was renamed the Rolls-Royce Trent when design began in 1988 and was the most powerful conventional aero-engine in production, being specified for the McDonnell Douglas MD11, the Airbus A330 and the Boeing 777, and on offer for the 440-passenger MD12.

The RB211 was largely a 'Derby' engine and Patchway's main activity through the seventies and eighties was centred around the Pegasus, the Olympus in various versions and the RB199 which was used to power the multi-role Tornado aircraft. Like the Olympus programme for Concorde, the RB199 was produced by an international consortium consisting of Rolls-Royce (40%), MTU (40%) and Fiat (20%), although the basic design was that of Rolls. Called Turbo-Union when it was formed in October 1969, the consortium collected orders for over 24,000 engines and production lasted well into the nineties. The RB199 proved a steady work load at Patchway throughout the seventies and eighties and there was a spin off of sub-contracts for many concerns. Among these on the design side was the Bristol based SAC Engineering. This company was one of the success stories of Bristol industry throughout this period with a wide range of aero-engineering expertise.

The Prime Minister, the Rt Hon. Margaret Thatcher M.P. arriving at Filton on an A320 of BA in 1990.
She is greeting the author. The Chairman of BAe, Professor Roland Smith is on the left and the
Chief Constable of Avon and Somerset, David Shattock, C.B.E., on the right.

The unique Pegasus vectored-thrust turbo-fan solved the problem of short or vertical take-off (STVOL) for fixed-wing aircraft and we have already seen how Hooker, Camm and Verdon-Smith saved the engine from cancellation. It first ran as long ago as 1959 and entered service a decade later in the Hawker-Siddeley Harrier VSTOL fighter. In the seventies, Hawker Siddeley and McDonnell Douglas formed a consortium to produce aircraft for both countries and a variety of Pegasus versions followed. The versatile Harrier can operate from small spaces such as the deck of a medium-sized ship and this ability enabled the Royal Navy to maintain its airpower long after the last conventional aircraft carrier had gone to scrap. In particular, the Harrier proved itself the match of conventional fighters in the 1982 Falklands War with Argentina and without it the expeditionary force which sailed to recover the islands would not have succeeded. The Pegasus remained in production at Patchway throughout the eighties, employing a substantial workforce and ranking as one of Bristol's greatest achievements.

Meanwhile, the Conservative Government had included Rolls in its privatisation programme but this took longer than expected as Sir Francis Toombs, Rolls' Chairman insisted on the write-off of outstanding debts. The Company finally went private in 1987. In 1986, Roll-Royce joined yet another consortium which could in due course prove critical to the future of the Bristol engine plant. This was Eurojet, set up with FiatAvio of Italy, MTU of Germany and ITP of Spain, to design and manufacture the engine to power the new European Fighter Aircraft (EFA). Designated EJ200, the engine is due to be rated at 20,000lb thrust. But by 1993, the effects of the European depression and the results of the end of the Cold War had caused Germany in particular to have second thoughts. Already the Patchway workforce was down to 6500 from its 1965 level of 21,000 and the loss of the EJ200 would have been a death blow to Patchway.

The personal intervention of Prime Minister John Major was needed to keep the project alive, albeit with reduced orders and extended timetable but this incident alone was sufficent to show that the way ahead was uncertain. The Guided Weapons Division factory at Filton also saw retrenchment throughout the eighties during which time it produced the Rapier surface-to-air defence missile which sold to a number of countries, and also Sea Wolf, an anti-missile missile for naval use. The division also expanded into the space industry. This later led to a profitable business in communications satellites and in particular to the Giotto space craft which intercepted Halley's Comet in 1986.

The Guided Weapons Division (by then called Dynamics Division) was amalgamated into the B.Ae Naval Weapons Division on 1 May 1985 and production of guided weapons ended at Filton in 1989.

Sir Reginald Verdon-Smith died on 21 June 1992 and a memorial service was held in St Mary Redcliffe, Bristol's finest church, on 22 July. Many civic and industry friends attended and the great church, which Verdon-Smith had served as churchwarden, was full to capacity. As the congregation left, two R.A.F. Harriers flew past in salute – the aircraft that Verdon-Smith had saved for the industry and the nation. To at least one onlooker it was as if the spirit of Bristol aviation had passed with them.

Throughout the remaining years of the 1990s, the Filton plant continued its commitment to the Airbus programme with design work, the supply of wing components and a busy programme of refurbishment and modification of earlier Airbus machines. The Patchway engine plant in similar manner continued to be a vital part of the Rolls-Royce production pattern.

Then, as the century turned and Filton celebrated the ninetieth anniversary of aircraft work starting on the site, two events in July 2000 seemed to be full of historic consequence.

The Farnborough Air Show in the millennium year was moved from the traditional September date to July and opened on the 24th of that month with an announcement from Airbus that it was to go into production with the Airbus 3XX, a giant, double-deck monster with a capacity of up to 600 passengers. Two airlines, Emirates and Air France, immediately announced firm orders scheduled for airline service in 2005. Filton would play its usual role of design and manufacture of wing components. The way ahead for European civil aviation was clear.

Within 24 hours of the announcement of the first A3XX orders, the European aircraft industry suffered a severe blow to its prestige when a Toulouse-built Concorde of Air France, Flight No. AF4590, crashed just after take-off from Paris Charles de Gaulle Airport on 25 July, killing all 109 passengers and crew and five persons on the ground in a hotel demolished by the wrecked machine. Worldwide shock was followed by a rush to judgement by the media who foresaw the end of Concorde services as a result. No Concorde

An impression of the giant Airbus 3XX in flight.

had crashed before and the aircraft had acquired a safety record unmatched until now. At the time of wriing Concorde's future remains uncertain.

The year 2010 will see the completion of the first century of Bristol aviation. By that time, the Airbus 3XX will have been in service for half a decade, paving the way towards more rewards (and heartaches!) in the second century of this remarkable industry.

ACKNOWLEDGEMENTS

The author joined the staff of the Bristol Aeroplane Company on 17 September 1947 as an engineering apprentice and served at Filton for over forty years. Much of the the narrative of this book is based on personal experience, aided by the recollections and help of many former colleagues, to whom he is most grateful.

Particular mention must be made of the late Sir Reginald Verdon-Smith who kindly gave the author his time and recollection as did the late Sir Archibald Russell. Chris Geoghean, present Managing Director at Filton, Howard Berry, Mrs Penny Telling, and chief photographer David Charlton, all of British Aerospace plc, supplied much information and many photographs. The staff of Clifton Pro-Lab, Bristol, restored many old photographs to useable form. All photographs are by courtesy of British Aerospace unless otherwise stated.

The author is also grateful to David Woolmington, Walter Gibb, Fred Burnell, Fred Price, Roy Jones, Professor Martin Lowson, Harold Lewis, Brian Howe, Derek Frise, Peter Pavey, Mr and Mrs Oliver Dearden, Hugh Metcalfe, John Cleverdon and George Ganley. The staffs of the Central Library, City of Bristol and of the Library of the University of Bristol were extremely helpful at all times.

Finally, thanks must be offered to Sir George White, the fourth baronet and great-grandson of the founder of the Bristol Aeroplane Company, who kindly checked the manuscript and made many helpful suggestions, and the author's family who have been as supportive as ever. I am grateful to them all.

Robert Wall   Bristol - 2000.

BIBLIOGRAPHY

Barnes, C.H.,	*Bristol Aircraft since 1910*	Putnam 1963
Bowyer, Chaz,	*Bristol Blenheim*	Ian Allen 1984
Brett, R. Dallas,	*History of British Aviation 1908-1914*	Private 1933
Bruce, J.M.,	*Aeroplanes of the Royal Flying Corps*	Putnam 1982
Bruce, J.M.,	*Britain's First Warplanes*	Arms & Armour 1987
Gardner, Charles,	*British Aircraft Corporation*	Batsford 1981
Green, G.,	*Bristol Aerospace since 1910*	Private 1985
Gunston, W.,	*By Jupiter–the life of Sir Roy Fedden*	1978
Harvey etc. ed.,	*Studies in the Business History of Bristol*	Bristol Academic Press 1982
Hobbs, Jack,	*Bristol Helicopters*	Frenchay 1984
Hooker, Sir Stanley,	*Not much of an engineer*	Airlife 1984
James, Ian,	*The story of Lulsgate Bottom*	Redcliffe 1989
Luff, David,	*Bulldog*	Airlife 1987
Knight, Geoffrey,	*Concorde – the inside story*	Weidenfeld 1976
Oxley, Charles,	*Bristol – the quiet survivor*	Private 1988
Pegg, Bill,	*Sent Flying*	MacDonald 1959
Pudney, John,	*Bristol Fashion*	Private 1960
Randall, Richard,	*Death of a Giant*	Downend Loc. Hist .1991
Russell, D.A.,	*The Book of Bristol Aircraft*	Harborough 1945
Russell, Sir Archibald,	*A Span of Wings*	Airlife 1992
Wakefield, K.,	*Target Filton*	rep. Redcliffe 1990
Wall, Robert,	*Airliners*	Collins 1981
Wixey, Kenneth,	*Parnall Aircraft since 1914*	Putnam 1990

Further sources include:
Newspapers -
The Times
Financial Times
Western Daily Press
Bristol Evening Post
Bristol Evening World
Periodicals -
Flight
The Aeroplane
R.AeS. Journal

SELECT INDEX